BAPTISED BY FIRE

BAPTISED BY FIRE

The Life of Smith Wigglesworth

Jack Hywel-Davies

HODDER AND STOUGHTON
LONDON SYDNEY AUCKLAND

First published in Great Britain in 1982
by Hodder and Stoughton Limited,
a division of Hodder Headline PLC

The right of Jack Hywel Davies to be identified as the author of
the Work has been asserted by him in accordance with the
Copyright, Designs and Patents Act 1988.

10 9 8 7 6

British Library Cataloguing in Publication Data

Hywel-Davies, Jack
Baptised by fire: the life of Smith
Wigglesworth.—(Hodder Christian
paperbacks).
1. Wigglesworth, Smith   2. Evangelists—
Great Britain—Biography
I. Title
269'.2'0924   BV3785.W482

ISBN 0 340 40740 9

Printed and bound in Great Britain by
Cox & Wyman Ltd, Reading, Berkshire

Hodder and Stoughton Ltd
A Division of Hodder Headline PLC
338 Euston Road
London NW1 3BH

This book is dedicated to three lovely ladies:

Alice, my mother, whose own life of faith was an invaluable foundation for my life;

Elsie, my wife and partner for thirty years – without her this book would not have been written;

Joan, my present wife, who continued the work, inspiring, encouraging and advising, especially in moments of despair.

I owe, not for this book alone, more than words can tell of gratitude to God for giving me three beautiful women.

Contents

Acknowledgments

It would not be possible to list all the people who have assisted me in the many and varied ways required to write a book, especially where background details are hard to find. However, some people must be mentioned, because without them this book would not have been written.

First, my good and valued friend Edward England. I do not know why Edward asked me to write this book. He was then with Hodder and Stoughton and I was with Kingsway Publications. We were standing beside my first wife Elsie's sick bed in our Eastbourne home when he suggested I write the life story of Smith Wigglesworth. Elsie quickly supported him. He was one of the 'few' to know that Elsie's condition was terminal, so maybe he thought a 'dose of Wigglesworth's faith' would do me good – and indeed it did. The writing of this book has made a deep impact on my inner self – faith's germinating ground.

Second, my wife Joan who has read the manuscript, helped me to 'communicate' better, corrected my English (she teaches it!) and kept me going when I would have given up.

Then there follows a whole host of others: Faith Campbell (daughter of Stanley Frodsham), who not only made valuable comments on the early manuscript but also directed me to other sources of information, in particular, the archives of the Assemblies of God Headquarters in Springfield, Missouri. Dr Thomas Zimmerman, for 'opening the doors' to the archives; and the Rev Wayne Warner and his assistant, who welcomed me 'inside'. Without these four this book would have been so much poorer.

Thanks also go to the Rev Leslie Wigglesworth, for new

insights into his grandfather's thinking; the Rev Alfred Missen, for access to the early publications of the Pentecostal pioneers, especially the priceless copies of *confidence*; and the Rev Desmond Cartwright, who provided valuable 'leads' for my research.

Finally, who can do without secretaries? I have always been blessed with the best. Two of whom, Liz Paisley and June Miles, not only transcribed my nearly illegible notes and erratic dictation, but also gave me opinions of considerable worth.

I cannot forget my fellow writers and their publications. Six deserve special mention: the late Stanley Frodsham, without his book *Apostle of Faith* many accounts of Smith Wigglesworth would have been lost; the late Dr David du Plessis, for his detailed account of Wigglesworth's prophecy; Dr Barry Chant, for his detailed and informative book on the Australian Pentecostal movement, *Heart of Fire*; the late Donald Gee, for his classic history of *The Pentecostal Movement*; Dr James Worsfold for his *A History of the Charismatic Movements in New Zealand*; and the Rev Wayne Warner for his fascinating chapter on Wigglesworth in his book entitled *Revival*.

Last, but by no means least, I thank the man many writers forget to mention, and someone who has become another friend, David Wavre, Director of Religious Books for Hodder and Stoughton. He not only took up the task of keeping me to mine where Edward England left off but also gave me valuable advice.

Jack Hywel-Davies

Foreword

I first heard of Smith Wigglesworth 26 years ago, when Jack Hywel-Davies was trying to persuade me to publish an article about what he called the 'New Pentecostalism'. It *was* published – he tells the story in this book – and it was the first many Christians in Britain knew of what we now call the Charismatic movement.

Smith Wigglesworth, of course, was not part of that movement. He had died long before it came on the scene. But back in the nineteen-thirties he had prophesied that the 'old churches' would one day accept the message and experience of Pentecostalism, and go on beyond what the old-style Pentecostalists had achieved. That seemed unlikely, to say the least, at a time when Pentecostalism was truly on the fringe of the life of the Churches, mainly confined to mission halls and preached by travelling evangelists like Aimee Semple Macpherson. Yet it has happened, exactly as he predicted, and today the charismatic movement, a lineal descendant of the 'old' Pentecostalism, is a powerful force in all the great Christian communions, from the Roman Catholic Church to the great Churches of the Reformation. It has attained ecclesiastical respectability, and yet its distinguishing marks are precisely those of the Pentecostal movement which Smith Wigglesworth helped to shape in the early years of this century: a 'second blessing' experience of the Holy Spirit, often called 'the baptism in the Spirit', and accompanying or following it various 'gifts of the Spirit' – speaking in tongues, prophecy, exorcism and healing.

It is the modern development which makes this biography of Wigglesworth not only fascinating – the story of a character of such eccentricity, excess and excitement could hardly be less than fascinating – but also highly topical. It is easy to forget how relatively 'new' a phenomenon Pentecostalism is in the Christian Church. Of course, the phenomena associated with it are described as present in the early Church, and various of them have surfaced or been reported at different times in Church history, but so far as can be told there was no coherent movement based on what one might call Pentecostal theology until the events described in this book, around the turn of the last century, brought into being a distinct and distinctive movement. One of its founders, the Reverend Alexander Boddy, vicar of a parish in Sunderland, remained in the Anglican ministry all his life, but most of the others were like Wigglesworth, who never actually 'joined' a church at all, but became instrumental in founding many, and especially helping to promote the work of the two main Pentecostalist denominations, the Assemblies of God and the Elim Church (to give them their British titles).

The truth is that any denomination would have had a problem comprehending a man like Wigglesworth, and this slightly eccentric individuality, together with an almost arrogant certainty about the rightness not only of his beliefs but also his practices, has often marked religious enthusiasts. He is not, as his sympathetic biographer portrays him, an immensely likeable man, but it is hard not to admire his courage, his simple mindedness and his faith. This man knew what it was to move mountains.

He also knew what it was to be regarded as a miracle-worker. Although his daughter was deaf and he suffered for much of his life from very poor eye-sight, he confidently claimed miracles of healing in the lives of other people who came to him. Many are recounted in this book, some with considerable detail about the circumstances. They may stretch the reader's credulity at times, but unless one takes the position that miracles can *never* occur it is hard to resist the feeling that Wigglesworth possessed, or was given, remarkable powers of healing. It is hard to imagine that a reputation like his, in the era of sceptical press coverage, could have grown up and been maintained unless it had some basis in fact.

He made no claim to be a theologian, and some of his attempts at theology, related in this book, show how wise was this modesty. But he had a vivid, memorable way of preaching, based on an unquestioning faith, and he loved to 'take God at his word'. He was not, it seems, a naturally modest man, but he gave the glory to God, and no one ever accused him of using the gifts he believed God had given him to line his own pockets or promote his own reputation. He founded no movement, launched no new denomination. He lived and died a blunt, straightforward Christian, 'ordinary' in the sense that he made no special claims for himself, but extraordinary both in his personal impact, and in his role as one player in a remarkable religious drama, the story of the modern charismatic renewal.

DAVID WINTER
Former Head of Religious Broadcasting
British Broadcasting Corporation

Preface

Jesus' choice of a man

In the latter part of the 1960s a well-known Anglican minister and I were involved in a programme for students in southeast London. He was, and still is, an energetic campaigner for good causes. At that time he had a very large parish in an area that was, in my opinion, a spiritual wilderness. It was also materially poor. So in addition to his praying he decided to do something else about it. And being the possessor of an organisational-type brain, one day he shut himself in his study and began with a blank sheet of paper.

He drew up a five-year plan. He did not expect instant success.

Part of his plan was to enlist a team of highly talented young clerics, preferably from the world of sport and Oxbridge, for a five-year programme to persuade the 'man in the street' to become the 'man in the church'. This clergyman was not short of qualifications himself. He was no mean runner, an Olympic athlete and well known in the media. His connections were impeccable and of considerable value to our student programme.

From a human point of view, he had all the ingredients for success. But after the five years were over, he had the courage to admit failure. And this he did in one of the leading Sunday newspapers.

With no disrespect for my Anglican friend's intentions, I compare his story with that of Jesus, another man with a mission.

He was, is, and always will be concerned with the plight of this world. And one day half-way through the last century he called a little Yorkshire boy who was pulling up turnips in a neighbouring farmer's field in the cold, cold winter to be a member of his team.

This boy was also a good runner. He also had a fine physique. But he did not qualify for Oxbridge, nor even for his grammar school. You see, his parents could not afford to send him to school, so he could neither read nor write.

But that did not deter Jesus. He took the boy as he was. Then over the succeeding years he gave him special equipment. Mark you his training wasn't in a classroom. We could call it field training. It was experiential, as some educationalists call it. Then he was sent by Jesus not only to London's south but all over the world.

He turned towns upside down. He left people either 'mad or glad' – never indifferent – no one could afford to ignore him. His main passion was to stir up in people an ever-increasing faith in God. And this is my ambition for this book, because it is his life story. It is a story of a life *Baptised by Fire – The Life of Smith Wigglesworth.*

1 First impressions

The paradoxical Apostle of Faith

He was a stockily-built man of medium height; he had the stance of a fighter, and a gruff voice unused to spare words. He meant business. He was a tough, forthright Yorkshireman, and he had a job to do.

My few encounters with him were from behind. That is, he was at the speaker's rostrum and I was seated on the back row of the platform. That suited me. I think it would have suited the devil too. But Smith Wigglesworth would have none of that: he faced his enemy, and the devil was enemy number one to him.

I had a ringside seat for some of Smith Wigglesworth's battles. The first was at London's historic Sion College,[1] a scene of many of his spiritual fights. I watched from the rear of the platform as, with the smallest of New Testaments in the biggest of workaday hands, he announced his intention of demolishing the devil's devices by the power given to him by the Holy Spirit.

Though highly polished in his appearance – a very neatly dressed man – he was unpolished in his speech. This coupled with his gruffness of voice and abruptness with questions, frightened those who did not know him. He was called the Apostle of Faith and you certainly needed a good measure of faith to approach him! Yet he could be as tender as a child. He was a compassionate man and was frequently seen crying over a deformed baby. He was a living paradox.

Defeating the devil's works

His approach to sickness was physical. From my ringside seat
at Sion College, I once saw him push a frail crippled lady who
had come to him for healing. After asking her to describe her
trouble, he barked, 'Do you believe God can heal you?' 'Yes,'
was her somewhat faltering reply. He prayed, commanded
the sickness to leave her body, then gave her the order,
'Walk.' Hesitatingly she began to walk. Then he pushed her.
As she hobbled into a run, he followed her down the centre
aisle shouting, 'Run woman, run.' She managed to gain some
strength to run and keep out of his reach. But Wigglesworth,
with arms akimbo and legs apart, stood in the aisle
thundering like Thor, 'Run woman, run.' She eventually
reached the exit and ran out into London's busy streets,
apparently healed as well as frightened. I was told that the
next man in the healing line quickly rediagnosed his sickness
from a stomach ulcer to a mild headache!

Smith Wigglesworth looked on all disease as the work of
the devil, so he was not averse to dealing with it by physical
force. But it was the disease rather than the victim that was
the subject of his attack. This, however, was not always
understood.

Mrs Blodwen Bell, the wife of the renowned Welsh gospel
singer Willie Llewellyn-Bell (an associate of Welsh evangelist
Stephen Jeffreys, also gifted in the healing ministry), once
visited Wigglesworth in his Yorkshire home. Noticing her
strange head movements, he asked her what was her trouble.
'I have a stiff neck,' she replied. 'I must have sat in a cold
draught of air when coming here in the train.' 'Do you want to
be healed?' he asked. 'I certainly do,' she replied. Whereupon
Wigglesworth hit her neck with the palm of his hand,
commanding the sickness to leave her. The force of the blow
brought tears to her eyes, and her husband remonstrated with
Wigglesworth. 'Brother,' responded Wigglesworth, 'if you
could see the evil of sickness as I see it, you wouldn't worry
about a few tears in your wife's eyes.'

Wigglesworth's usual approach to a sick person was to charge at him and then strike the relevant part of his body. When questioned about this by his grandson, Leslie Wigglesworth, he explained that to him all sickness came from the devil and he hated every expression of it. He loved the sick but hated their affliction. He would frequently say in defence of his unusual methods, 'Fear looks, faith jumps.' And jump he did, irrespective of the petitioners.

On one occasion, when he was conducting a 'healing mission' in Oakland, California, two sisters heard about this strange Englishman who seemed to possess remarkable powers of healing. They were not Christians and knew little about the Bible. Their brother was a patient in a nearby hospital and was desperately ill. Looking for a miracle they arranged for him to be taken by stretcher and ambulance to one of the meetings. 'Please be gentle with him,' they pleaded, 'he is very, very ill.' Wigglesworth either did not hear their request or decided to carry on in his usual manner regardless. He approached the man on the stretcher and in a loud voice commanded the sickness to come out of the man, hitting him squarely in the stomach. The man passed out. One of the sisters became hysterical, shouting, 'You've killed him. You've killed him. Call the police.' They rushed the unconscious man back to hospital. After a few hours he regained consciousness. When he did, he was found to be completely healed.

A man with a mission

Wigglesworth was a fearless pioneer prophet who didn't for one moment care about himself. He believed he was commissioned by God to preach the good news of Jesus and that all the resources of the Holy Spirit were at his disposal. He entered into his task in the only way he knew, and if people misunderstood him it was their fault for failing to discover what his mission was all about. He possessed

complete and utter faith in God and his word. It was a
childlike simplicity; as St Paul wrote, 'God has deliberately
chosen to use ideas the world considers foolish and of little
worth in order to shame those people considered by the world
as wise and great' (1 Cor 1:27, Living Bible). And these words
surely applied to Wigglesworth.

Only believe

What motivated this uneducated Yorkshire plumber? He
repeatedly said that his main purpose in life was to get people
to increase their faith in God. Once when he was preaching in
Pudsey, Yorkshire, in a tiny Pentecostal mission room,
following a preaching tour of Europe (in 1925), he said: 'I find
so many people trying to help themselves. What God wants is
an "absolute cling" to him ... God has got only one grand plan
for us – only believe ... You are brought into everything God
has for you because you dare only believe what he says ...
God would have me to press into your heart this living truth –
only believe, absolute rest, perfect tranquillity, where God is
absolutely taking charge of the whole situation ... Are you
ready to sing now?' He then invited the congregation to sing,
as he did in all his meetings, the chorus he made his own:

> Only believe, only believe,
> All things are possible, only believe.
> Only believe, only believe,
> All things are possible, only believe.

But Smith always interposed an 'h' as he thundered out 'only
believe'. And he would spell it out 'h-o-n-e-l-y'. After the
same fashion, he would refer to his daughter Alice as 'Halice'
and, conversely, his son Harold as 'Arold'.

'I am out for men,' he would say. 'It's my business to make
everybody hungry, dissatisfied, hungry for God. It's my
business to make people either mad or glad. I must have every

man filled with the Holy Spirit. I must have a message from heaven that will not leave people as I found them.'

So let us have a closer look at the life and work of this remarkable Yorkshireman – Smith Wigglesworth.

Note

[1]Sion College is located on the Thames Embankment in London near Blackfriars Bridge. It was founded over three hundred years ago by Dr Thomas White, when he was vicar of St Dunstan's of Fleet Street, as a place where clergy could 'maintain love by conversing together'. In the years before the Second World War its baronial-style hall was rented by Howard Carter's Pentecostal Bible School for Friday night meetings when Pentecostal leaders from widely scattered parts of the world would 'drop-in' unannounced and be invited to the platform to preach. No doubt the good doctor did not envisage a Smith Wigglesworth 'maintaining love' in this manner!

2 'Six o'clock will always come my son'

A Yorkshire childhood

Smith Wigglesworth was born on June 10th 1859 and baptised in the nearby Anglican church on December 4th of the same year. His parents were John and Martha Wigglesworth, who had four children – three sons and one daughter. Theirs was a poor family and they lived in a small Yorkshire village named Menston. So small was the village that even today the traveller would find it difficult to locate on his map. It was in that rugged and honest Yorkshire countryside, an hour's walk from Ilkley Moor, that Smith spent his first few years.

The song which made Ilkley Moor famous, 'On Ilkla Moor baht'at' (i.e. 'On Ilkley Moor without a hat') is said to have been composed in 1886 by a Halifax church choir enjoying a picnic on the moor. And Haworth Parsonage, the place where two of the greatest English novels, *Jane Eyre* and *Wuthering Heights* were written, was within walking distance of Menston. It was also the home of the Rev William Grimshaw, who was a close friend of John Wesley and became one of his early preachers.

Wigglesworth was raised in surroundings renowned for their craggy edges and wooded ravines. A county marked with the work of ancient peoples over three thousand years and more ago. During Smith's early life Menston was an important inland spa and residential centre. But the Wigglesworths were not to receive any of these benefits.

Family life

John Wigglesworth worked long hours for little pay, digging deep ditches in the middle of winter. His wife often suggested waiting until the weather eased for the ground to thaw. However, such was their plight that Smith's father had to work, whatever the weather, to provide the bare necessities for his family's existence.

One day when the frost was heavy and the ground hard, John Wigglesworth's shovel threw up a spadeful of soft wet clay. A robin suddenly appeared, picked up a worm, and flew to a nearby tree to enjoy his meal. Then the robin rendered a 'song of thanksgiving'. Leaning back on his shovel, John said to young Smith, 'If that robin can sing like that for a worm, surely I can work like a father for your mother, you and your sister and brothers.'

The Wigglesworth family were great lovers of nature. John Wigglesworth could describe and name all the birds of the district. At one time he had as many as sixteen song birds in their home. Smith caught the 'nature disease' from his father and spent all his spare time in the fields surrounding his village looking for birds' nests and watching the fledglings grow. On one occasion he found a nest full of fledglings and, under the impression that they had been abandoned, took them home. To his surprise, the birds' parents found the youngsters and would fly to Smith's bedroom to feed them. So the thrush and the lark became his friends, and both in his country walks and in his home he developed a close relationship with them. This closeness with nature stimulated a desire to be close to its creator. Smith always wanted to know God from these early years. He once told his friend Stanley Frodsham that even in a storm when he was enveloped in thunder and fire-like lightning, he could talk to God about it with a simple faith.

Although the Wigglesworth children were blessed with good, hard-working and honest parents who did not profess to be Christians, nevertheless they brought up their children to reverence God.

Early working life

When he was six years old, Smith took his first job. He worked for a nearby farmer, pulling and cleaning turnips in his fields. It was a hard life working from morning until night with some meagre school lessons between.

A variety of industries dominated the economic life of Yorkshire. One of the most productive was the woollen industry. It had the monopoly in the production of worsted cloths which were sold worldwide. The early development of this trade was due in part to the rearing of sheep on the moors and to an abundance of hydraulic power. The nearby city of Bradford specialised in yarns and mixed worsted cloth, so there were many opportunities for work in the mills. It was there that John found employment as a weaver. He was also able to obtain work for Smith, who at that age possessed a better physique than most boys. So it was that Smith started work in the mill, his second job, at the tender age of seven.

With his father, brother and himself working, things at home became easier and food was more plentiful. Martha Wigglesworth, a hard-working woman, made the clothes for her family, which were often supplemented by those given to her by friends. Smith used to say that it was quite common for him to wear an overcoat with sleeves four inches too long, though this turned out to be a blessing in disguise in the cold Yorkshire winters. Six days a week, his day started at five o'clock, in order to begin work in the mill at six and did not end until six in the evening. One day a very tired Smith said to his father, 'It's a long time from six while six in t'mill.' With tears in his eyes, his father replied, 'Well, six o'clock will always come my son.'

3   Only believe

Conversion in a Methodist church

Grandmother Wigglesworth was one of the early Methodists; she used to take Smith to the little chapel in Menston – John Wesley had preached there during the previous century and it is still standing today.

At the early age of eight Smith was attracted to these simple and earnest Yorkshire folk who enjoyed their worship without inhibitions. They thought nothing of time; in fact, in spite of the long working days of the week, they were to be heard in their little chapel at seven o'clock on a Sunday morning singing praises to their Lord.

On one such occasion, when young Smith was present with his grandmother, the small congregation sang these words:

> The Lamb, the Lamb, the bleeding Lamb,
>   The Lamb of Calvary.
> The Lamb that was slain
> That liveth again, to intercede for me.

It was no mournful dirge, rather it was a song of rejoicing, and these Methodists were exuberant in their joy as they danced around the coal-fired stove which was blazing away in the middle of their barn-like meeting room. The words took hold of Smith as he saw that Christ was that Lamb, and that he had also died for him. As the realisation of sins forgiven and a new life from heaven dawned on eight year old Smith, he also joined in the dancing and singing, clapping his hands to the rhythm of the tune.

'I knew that day that I had received a new life which had come from God,' he later said. 'I was born again. I saw that God wants us so badly that he has made the condition as simple as he possibly could – only believe.' And those two words were to become evangelist Smith Wigglesworth's stock-in-trade for the rest of his life as he preached to congregations in some of the world's largest cities.

However, his schooling was badly neglected. A twelve-hour working day for a lad of such tender years left no time for his education. Recalling those days in later years he would say, 'The longer I lived, the more I thought. But the less language I had at my disposal to express those thoughts.' He was not unlike his mother in that respect. She could never relate an event to her family intelligibly, leaving them so confused that her husband would have to intervene, 'Nay mother, you'll have to begin again.'

Early attempts at speaking in public

One of the features of early Methodism was the class meeting. As early as 1738, these meetings were introduced by John Wesley when he decided to divide his followers into small bands. This enabled them to speak 'freely and plainly to each other as to the "real state" of their hearts'. Wesley advised them, in face of strong opposition from leaders of the state church, to 'strengthen one another and talk together' as often as possible because 'all the world was against them'. He encouraged them to give their testimonies in these meetings, sharing their difficulties and their successes with complete honesty. This is a practice used in group therapy these days but, sadly, not followed by the majority of churches.

Young Smith would sometimes stand in these meetings and, after a great deal of hesitation, try to find the right words to express himself, only to end in confusion and tears. After one such occasion three old men in the group felt constrained to lay hands on the lad and pray for him. Although he continued to have difficulty with his public speaking, their prayers had a marked effect upon his personal life. 'The Spirit of the Lord came upon me and I was instantly set free from my bondage,' he said. 'I not only believed but I could speak.' But this was only on a one-to-one basis. However, from that time on he was possessed by a burning desire to talk about the Christian faith to everyone he met. 'From the time of my conversion I became a soul-winner,' he would say. 'And the first person I won for Christ was my own dear mother.'

Confirmation in the Church of England

John Wigglesworth was not a churchgoer, but he did have a great respect for the Church of England, largely on account of his liking for the Rev B J Hughes, the local curate, who used to join him for a pint of ale in the village coaching inn. So John decided his sons should support the parish church even though he was not a member. It was not long before the church organist enlisted the Wigglesworth brothers in the church choir, and although Smith could not read he had an alert mind and soon learnt the words and the tunes of the hymns and chants. He must have made a good impression on the curate, as well as the vicar of the senior church in Burley-on-Wharfedale, because he was soon selected for confirmation by the bishop.

Confirmation in the Church of England is one of the sacramental rites by which the confirmee, after being instructed in the doctrines of the Christian faith, is admitted to full membership of the church. The rite has been practised from the days of the early church and includes the laying-on of hands by the bishop for the sealing of the Holy Spirit. There has always been great variety in this practice, depending on the theological stance of the bishop. But wherever this rite is adopted it is claimed that it follows the example of the apostles 'in order to claim our Lord's promise to send the Holy Spirit to strengthen the church'.

For us, as we consider the life of Smith Wigglesworth, who was to become one of the fathers of the Pentecostal movement, the coincidence between the intentions and teachings of the early Anglicans and those of this century's Pentecostalists is striking. At the time, of course, young Smith Wigglesworth knew nothing of this, indeed the Pentecostal movement was yet to be born, but here he was, an illiterate boy from a poor Yorkshire cottage, at three o'clock on a Thursday afternoon (September 5th 1872), in All Saints Church, Otley, Yorkshire, kneeling before the dignified bishop in his full ecclesiastical regalia. 'When the bishop laid his hands on me,' recalled Smith Wigglesworth later in life, 'I had a similar experience to the one I had forty years later when I was baptised in the Holy Spirit. My whole body was filled with the consciousness of God's presence, a consciousness that remained with me for days. After the confirmation service all the other boys were swearing and quarrelling, and I wondered what had made the difference between them and me.'

4 New beginnings – home, job, things spiritual

Bradford

It was also in 1872, when Smith was thirteen, that John Wigglesworth decided it was time for them to move nearer to the woollen mills where there were better working opportunities. So the Wigglesworth family found themselves rehoused in the rapidly prospering town of Bradford (it was not made a city until 1897). Since the granting of its first markets in the thirteenth century Bradford had risen to be the world's leading wool-dealing centre and weaver of woollen fabrics. The first spinning factory was opened in 1798 and with the coming of the power loom in 1825 the town became a hive of commercial activity.

A Brethren influence

The move to Bradford was to have a profound impact on Smith's life. He soon found work in one of the woollen mills, and came under the influence of a godly man who belonged to the Christian Brethren (then called Plymouth Brethren). The Brethren were known for two special features: their emphasis on the teaching of the second coming of Christ and their fastidious attention to Bible study. They were, and still are, great Bible students. This encounter was to have a marked effect upon Wigglesworth's spiritual experience by giving him a firm foundation for his faith and a love for God's word. This man, who worked as a steam-fitter in the same mill as young Smith, took an instant liking to him. He taught him the skills of plumbing, which later was to take Wigglesworth into a successful and profitable business career. In addition to this valuable training, the steam-fitter would read and explain Bible passages to his young friend during their meal breaks.

One day the lunchtime conversation got around to water baptism. The Christian Brethren teach 'believers' baptism', which means that to be baptised the candidate must be old enough to understand its meaning. He was told that this ancient rite signified the burial of the old life, diseased by sin and consequently separating the individual from God, followed by a resurrection to a new life in Christ. This was new to Wigglesworth, but it did not take him long to accept this meaning for water baptism. Subsequently, at the age of seventeen, he was baptised for the second time, but this time at his own request and by total immersion in water.

Early attempts at evangelism

After the Wigglesworth family set up home in Bradford, Smith looked for a church which could provide an outlet for his evangelistic zeal. The nearby Church of England failed to do this. Soon he found his way back to the local Methodists who were very missionary-minded, and this suited Smith. They also arranged special meetings for young people where they were given an opportunity to engage in public speaking but this continued to be a difficulty for him. However, he found it easier to talk to the men and boys who worked alongside him in the mill about his faith in God. Inevitably there were rebuffs and he was ridiculed, though on his own admission he deserved some of them.

At this time two distinctive features emerged: one personal, the other habitual. He was not the most tactful of men, an unfortunate trait that was to dog his footsteps for the remainder of his life. The other habit, which he also retained, was to carry a New Testament wherever he went, even though at that time he couldn't read.

Smith and the Salvation Army

In 1875 William Booth visited Bradford and commenced a series of Christian meetings. Later these groups became known as the Salvation Army and were formed into individual corps.[1] Smith was immediately attracted to them with their dedication and zeal for witnessing to their saviour. He found their no-nonsense aggressive evangelism just 'up his street', and he began to attend their meetings. Although they did not accept the practice of 'believers' baptism', he remained with them because they were people of action. It also seemed to him that they had more power in their ministry than anybody else at that time. They would have whole nights of prayer, and many would be laid out on the floor of the hall under the power of the Holy Spirit, sometimes for as long as twenty-four hours at a time. It was also quite common for these early Salvationists to claim in faith from between fifty and a hundred 'souls for Christ' in a week. He then believed that this was the real evidence of spiritual power and not 'fleshly manifestations' (i.e. the result of human effort without God's power).

A plumber by trade

By the time he was eighteen Smith was well experienced in the craft of a plumber, so he decided to leave his work at the mill and better himself. Although he could neither read nor write, he was an intelligent lad and aware of the importance of a good personal appearance.

One day he set out to find a job in the plumbing business. He cleaned his shoes with an extra shine. He pressed his suit for the umpteenth time, donned a new clean shirt and a sparklingly white stiff collar, and presented himself at the home of the boss of one of Bradford's best plumbing firms. 'No. I don't need anyone else in my firm,' was the curt answer he got from the blunt Yorkshireman who came to the door. Not daunted, and wise enough to give a polite reply,

Wigglesworth said, 'Thank you sir. I'm sorry to have troubled you.' As Smith left the house and made his way down the path to the front gates, the businessman watched the retreating figure with increasing unease. 'He's a smart looking lad,' he said to himself. 'There's something about him that's different. I can't let him go.' Smith got the job. His first assignment was to fit a row of houses with water piping. He did it in a week. When he reported the job completed, his boss was astonished. 'It's impossible,' he said. 'No one has ever completed that amount of work in so short a time.' He examined the work and found it was perfect. Smith continued to work for this man, and he worked so fast that his employer found it difficult to keep him fully employed.

A fit witness

Smith was a keen cyclist. He not only enjoyed the experience, but placed great emphasis on keeping his body fit. George Stormont, at whose home in Leigh-on-Sea Smith was a frequent visitor, once told me that Wigglesworth was so fastidious about personal hygiene that after his daily bath he would tone himself up with a Swedish loofah. Although a firm believer in divine healing, he would not disregard any medical advice given him. On one occasion later in life, when he suffered from stones in his kidneys and gall bladder, he was told by a doctor that eggs were harmful to his condition. From that day onwards he never ate an egg.

The Yorkshire dales were on Wigglesworth's doorstep. Whenever he had time he would be found cycling through the villages and hamlets. The dales, which have some of the finest waterfalls to be seen, were a constant delight to him. The rushing of the waters at West Stonesdale Beck into the Swale in a series of magnificent falls is an inspiring sight and a place he regularly visited. Cycling alongside the river winding its way through the stony ravines where rocks rise like the walls of an old fortress would be for him a form of relaxation.

Ferns of rarest kinds, mosses and wildflowers were there in profusion. These were scenes for Smith that were both rich and gentle, and he would find pleasure in describing them in later years to his friends around the world. He rode these hills on his cycle with the powerful legs of an athlete. It was said that though using the high gear of his cycle he never had to walk up a Yorkshire hill because he was strong enough to ride it.

There was an added purpose in his cycling trips. He would always combine them with his personal witness. It was not uncommon for him to invite a Christian friend for a ten-day tour of the Yorkshire dales with the express purpose of persuading at least three people a day to become followers of Jesus Christ.

Unlike many of his fellow-Christians he took a keen interest in other outdoor activities, particularly cricket and bowls. He was a firm believer in keeping himself fit both mentally and physically as well as spiritually, so much so that later in life, when he travelled extensively, he was not averse to doing so in comfort, frequently using first-class facilities when he considered it beneficial to his health and subsequent ministry. He took care of his bodily health because he believed he was the custodian of special divine gifts. I recall the late Ernie Harford, of the Elim Pentecostal Church, telling a story of Wigglesworth's visit to a church in the Midlands when he was its pastor. Ernie was taking Smith by car to preach at the evening service, and was apparently driving a little too fast for Smith's comfort. Suddenly Ernie was conscious of his guest's hand on his shoulder, followed by the comment, 'Take care brother Harford, you have a piece of God's special property on board.'

Liverpool

Though his work for the Bradford plumber was proceeding satisfactorily, Smith decided to explore fresh fields for greater experience and increased financial reward. Hearing of better opportunities in the thriving city of Liverpool, he ventured into 'foreign country' crossing the natural barrier of the Pennines. In those days it was no small thing for a Yorkshireman to seek his fortune in Lancashire, even though the Wars of the Roses was well past.

Liverpool was one of the largest seaports in Britain. It was the exporting centre for the textiles of Lancashire and Yorkshire, but it also had a variety of other industries. It was a city with commercial connections to every port in the world, but mainly in North America. Ships plying between Liverpool and New York, Philadelphia, Boston, Baltimore, Galverston, New Orleans and many Canadian ports were commonplace. So the opportunities for a young, aspiring plumber were numerous and varied. Liverpool was highly active in those days, enjoying an enormous trade with the still young and growing countries of North America. Engineering works, especially those connected with marine navigation, were growing up on a large scale. Ship-building and ship-repairing were the order of the day. In addition, pottery and china manufacturers flourished, so it was inevitable that ambitious young men in the north of England, like Smith Wigglesworth, should seek their livelihood there.

However, in spite of its commercial success, Liverpool was also a city of the poor. They were exploited by the greed of the wealthy industrialists and possessed no organised social services to assist them. The city was a conglomerate of narrow alleys and treacherous slopes which in earlier times had been visited by the plague. In its seamy side it was a 'slum-palace' overrun by thieves and vagabonds, a sad place for those who lived on 'the wrong side of the track'.

This was the scene that confronted young Wigglesworth, who had been brought up in the evangelistic fervour of Methodism, Anglican puritanism and latterly the social and loving concern of the Salvation Army. He was twenty years old when he moved to Liverpool, but something happened to him in Bradford before he left that is not uncommon to men of that age. He 'noticed' a vivacious and pretty girl known to her friends as 'Polly'.

Note

[1] William Booth began his evangelistic work in a tent in Whitechapel, London, in 1865. It was then known as the Christian Revival Association. This was changed to the East London Christian Mission in 1870 and extended to cover all London. The title 'Salvation Army' was first used in a leaflet published by Booth in 1878, and it was soon accepted as the name of the whole movement.

5   Her name was Mary Jane but...

Although her friends called her 'Polly', she was born Mary Jane Featherstone to God-fearing parents who were devout Methodists. Despite her grandparents' wealth, Polly's father, who gave his spare time as a temperance lecturer, refused his inheritance because their fortune came from the sale of alcohol.

Polly moves to Bradford

In 1877, when Polly was seventeen, her father decided that she should have business experience, so he found a place for her to be trained as a milliner. But one month was as much as his spirited daughter could endure, and she ran away. Eventually she arrived in Bradford in an endeavour to find fame and fortune. Somewhat naïvely she found accommodation in a house of ill-repute, but through a chance encounter with someone who was aware of the risks of such a place she was helped to find somewhere more suitable to live.

She then began looking for employment and found a large family who needed domestic help. Now set free from the restraints of her strict upbringing, Polly set out to explore this large and fascinating place called Bradford. Life was good, and excitedly she continued her discoveries of what life was like in a big city.

A life-changing encounter

One day during an expedition into the city centre, her attention was caught by the sound of trumpets and drums. It came from the centre of a group of people in the market square, and soon curious Polly was pushing her way through the crowd to see what it all was about. It was an open-air evangelistic meeting. But there was something different about these happy young people. When they went marching along, blazing away on their trumpets, trombones and euphoniums, and banging enthusiastically on the big bass drum, Polly followed. She thought, 'Where are these silly people going?' But soon they reached their destination. It was a run-down theatre building which they had rented for their meetings. Though it was contrary to her upbringing to enter such a building, her curiosity got the better of her and she continued to follow. With a furtive glance around her, she quickly entered and found a corner seat in the balcony. These young and enthusiastic Christians were the nucleus of General William Booth's Salvation Army in Bradford, and Polly little realised what this chance encounter was to do to her life.

The evangelist for that evening's meeting was Tillie Smith, sister of the renowned evangelist Gypsy Smith. Both were friends of William Booth and conducted meetings in public halls throughout the country. As Tillie Smith preached about Christ and his power to forgive sins, Polly's young heart was strangely moved. Then came the invitation to the 'penitent form'. Polly was suddenly overcome by an uncomfortable sense of personal sin. She shifted uncomfortably in her seat, afraid to stay and fearful of going. Suddenly she rose to her feet, walked down the stairs and made her way across the lower floor to the penitent form. At first she knelt there weeping and resisting all attempts to help her. Eventually Tillie Smith came and knelt beside her. Gently and lovingly Tillie spoke to this attractive young woman, retelling the greatest love story ever written. There Polly found Jesus as her saviour. The change was dramatic. She leapt to her feet, threw her gloves in the air and shouted 'Hallelujah, it's done.'

How a friendship was born

Also at that meeting, sitting only a few seats away, was a

young man in his teens. When he heard the girl's spontaneous expression of praise his heart gave an extra beat. Later he told one of his friends that something strange happened inside him when he heard Polly's shout of joy, and from that moment he knew that she was to be 'his girl'. That could only have been an act of Smith's faith, for Smith Wigglesworth was that young man.

Polly was bright, intelligent and beautiful. Smith was shy, awkward and uneducated. But an intimate friendship soon developed. Polly made great strides in her spiritual life, and it was soon recognised by Tillie and her brothers Gypsy and Lawley (later to be a commissioner in the Salvation Army) that here was 'officer material'. One day, 'out of the blue', there came a summons from the General to present herself for an interview.

Polly moves to Leith

Word had got to him about this young woman in Bradford who was a fluent speaker and a born leader. When the General had completed his interview of Polly, he recognised that she was sufficiently talented and capable to be commissioned without the customary course of training. He thereupon invited her to become a Salvation Army officer and she accepted.

That was the beginning of a setback to her friendship with Smith Wigglesworth: officers only marry officers in the Salvation Army, furthermore, Smith was not even a 'soldier' because he refused to join the Army although he was one of its most ardent supporters. Then came the next blow. In the way that superior officers in any army have with their subordinates, the hierarchy of the Salvation Army 'arranged' for Polly to be posted to a new corps in the town of Leith, Scotland, some two hundred miles away. In those days that was comparable to being sent to New York.

Painful though the separation was to both of them, Polly's life in Leith proved to be a good training ground. Open-air meetings were a 'must' for all Salvationists, and these were considered fair game for the amusement of the local layabouts who would use anything at hand, from rotten tomatoes to bad eggs, to hurl at Officer Featherstone in the 'ring'. Some practical jokers would even heat pennies in a fire, and then throw them into the 'ring' at collection time, expecting to hear a string of oaths when they burnt the hands of the collectors. But they were disappointed when it came to Polly. She maintained a cool composure and continued to use her musical voice to sing and testify, sometimes in spite of collecting black eyes from rowdy drunks.

The Salvation Army trained their officers not only for public speaking but also to show personal interest in young converts. One of Polly's charges was a young wife living on the sixth floor of a tenement building in a poor area of Leith. As was often the case, this young woman's husband was strongly opposed to her attendance at the 'Army' meetings. Nor was he slow to use brute force to give emphasis to his demands. One day, on returning home, he found Polly in prayer with his wife. He became angry and threatened to throw Polly down the many flights of stairs if she did not stop praying. Undeterred, Polly prayed on. In a wild rage he lifted Polly from her knees and began carrying her down the stairs. But with every step he took Polly prayed, 'Lord save this man. Save his soul Lord.' Almost foaming at the mouth in his rage, the man continued to curse and swear with every step he took, but Polly prayed on. Then the miracle happened. As he put his foot on the last step, he broke down and wept, calling on Jesus for mercy. Together they knelt on that last step, a unique 'penitent form' and Polly gently and happily led the once-angry husband in the sinner's prayer.

The break with the Army

Discipline in the Salvation Army was very rigid, especially with its officers. This was particularly so where relationships with the opposite sex were concerned. Though a favourite with the 'General', Polly Featherstone was not treated any differently from her fellow officers, male or female. However, she was an attractive woman and was frequently the attention of male admirers: one of the Scottish 'soldiers' in particular was enamoured by her.

Her period of duty at Leith was coming to an end and, whether the soldier knew this or not, he began to reveal his amorous intentions to such an extent that it attracted the attention of Polly's superior officers. Then the inevitable happened. They summoned Polly to a meeting with them at which they closely questioned her about the Scotsman and her 'supposed love' for someone who was not an officer. In spite of her repeated denials of this charge, they refused to believe her. In desperation they resorted to the familiar escape route of many Christian leaders and said, 'Polly, let's pray about it.' However, they didn't bargain for Polly's prayer. She didn't wait for them to start praying, but blurted out as soon as they knelt down, 'Lord, you know that these men think I'm interested in a Scotsman. But you know I'm not. If what these Scots say about each other is true, they are all so mingy they would nip a currant in two if they could save the other half. But you know I don't believe that about them, as I've found them most kind. But please show my fellow officers that I don't intend to marry anyone here in Scotland.' And that ended her inquisition.

Little did her superiors realise, but her thoughts were with a young Yorkshire plumber now living in Liverpool with whom she began to recognise she was very much in love. That was the beginning of the end of her service with the Salvation Army. Very soon she returned to Bradford, resigned her commission, though she never lost her love for General Booth and the 'Army', and joined a new evangelistic group (Elizabeth Baxter's 'Blue Ribbon Army') that had established itself in Bradford along similar lines to the Salvation Army.

6 Smith Wigglesworth's first 'prophecy' fulfilled

Smith's evangelistic work in Liverpool

On his arrival in Liverpool, Smith Wigglesworth had attached himself to the Salvation Army. Here this reserved and outwardly hard Yorkshireman tried to find a way of expressing his concern for the poor of the bustling Lancashire seaport. But he was not prepared for the horrific scenes of poverty he found in Liverpool. Every town in England had its human 'refuse', but none had as much as Liverpool, where he seemed to encounter such people on almost every street corner. The Salvation Army in Liverpool operated a combination of spiritual and social concerns for these deprived people, so Wigglesworth energetically threw in his lot with the activities of the Liverpool corps.

Though thought by many to be hard and gruff, for that was how he came across, in reality Smith was affectionate and compassionate, particularly to children: 'I had a great desire to help the young people,' he once confided to a friend. Each week he would travel the streets of downtown Liverpool inviting scores of poorly clothed, shoeless, hungry and destitute boys and girls to a rented shed at the dockside. His employers admired his zeal and made the sheds available, and from his own earnings Smith would provide food for the children who came. Hundreds of them followed him like the rats that followed the Pied Piper of Hamlyn; they were not only given their first good meal but also heard the story of Jesus' love.

However, this did not fully satisfy Smith's need to show love to the people of this seaport district. He began a visitation programme to hospitals and ships. 'God gave me a great heart for the poor,' he said. 'I used to work hard and

spend all I had on them.' But even though he could talk freely
to individuals on a one to one basis, he still had difficulty in
addressing public meetings. The Salvation Army officers in
Liverpool would ask Smith to speak at their meetings
because they admired his work among children and the poor
but, though wanting to speak publicly, he would always end
broken and crying before the people.

When he was twenty-three, Smith returned to Bradford
and to his Polly. His intention was to open a business in his
own name and give all his spare time to evangelism. And this
he set about doing without delay.

Smith and Polly marry

His business prospered and before the year of 1882 was out,
Smith and Polly were married. He was twenty-three, she was
twenty-two. They were very much in love, and the 'prophecy'
he gave to his friend in the Salvation Army hall the night
Polly gave her life to Christ some five years earlier was
fulfilled. Their home in Victor Road, Bradford, was to
become known throughout the world as men and women
from all walks of life came to see this man and benefit from
his unique ministry.

In later years Smith, recalling his life with Polly, would say,
'All that I am today, I owe under God, to my precious wife.
She was lovely. She became a great help to me in my spiritual
life. She was always an inspiration to holiness. But she also
saw how ignorant I was, and immediately began to teach me
to read properly and to write. Unfortunately, she never
succeeded in teaching me to spell. She was also a great soul-
winner. I encouraged her to continue her ministry of
evangelising, and I continued my business as a plumber.'

The beginning of the Wigglesworths' 'Mission' in Bradford

His business took him to different parts of Bradford and soon he began to recognise the spiritual need of areas where there were no church buildings. He would talk to Polly about this when he returned home in the evenings. Encouraged by his wife he started to look for a suitable building to rent where together they could hold meetings. Very soon he found a convenient hall. But still Smith could not preach without breaking down. Because she was fluent and an experienced evangelist, Polly took charge of the meetings, while Smith would sit alongside her on the platform. However, when the people came forward in response to Polly's invitation Smith would be at the penitent form to pray with them. In his words, 'Polly's work was to put down the net, and mine to land the fish!'

At first they were extremely happy. Life together seemed to be perfect and they fitted into each other's lifestyle with ease. To their families and friends they appeared to be a perfect match – 'ideal makeweights'. What one lacked, the other had. And they prayed together about everything. They were endowed with five children who were 'covered' by prayer even before they were born: Alice, Seth (whose son Leslie became head of the Elim Missionary Society), Harold, Ernest and George. And Smith was a good father, looking after the children so that Polly could be free for her ministry. She continued to be successful in her public speaking engagements, not only in their 'Mission' but further afield, as reports of her work became more widely known. Smith, for his part, developed his plumbing enterprise in and around Bradford as he gained a reputation for high quality work and honesty in business dealings. His company became one of the most successful of its kind in Bradford and attracted an increasing volume of work. Smith was on the way to being a wealthy man.

Success leads to failure

This success began to interfere with his Christian life. So

much business came to him that it began to eat into his spare time. Consequently he had less and less time available to support Polly in their church work. During a particularly hard winter Smith and his employees were called upon to work long hours; in emergencies, this continued through the weekends. Business could not have been better, but the inroads it made into Wigglesworth's church life and subsequent personal spirituality proved highly disruptive. His wife, though aware of what was happening, continued with her ministry unchanged. Furthermore, it seemed that the colder he became to God and her, the warmer was she. No longer was he assisting her in their little church. She battled on alone. But matters were to grow worse, and Smith's slide into coldness and indifference began to affect their home life.

Always prone to abruptness, he now became verbally abusive. Returning home unusually late one evening from a weeknight service, Polly was met by a furious husband. 'I want you to know', bellowed Smith, 'that I am the master of this house. And I'm not going to have you coming home at so late an hour as this.' Polly recognised that this was not the man she married. He was under conviction. He knew he was out of God's will, and her continued devotion to her Christian work highlighted his backslidden condition. Polly refused to be rattled, and quietly replied, 'I know you are my husband, but Christ is my Master.' This further infuriated Smith. In uncontrolled anger, he took hold of Polly and opening the back door forcibly threw her out of the house. However, he hadn't bargained for Polly's tenacity. Going round the house, she discovered that the front door had been left unlocked. Without any fuss she promptly re-entered the house; seeing the funny side of it, she burst out laughing. In spite of his bad temper and irritability, Smith found himself laughing along with her.

Nevertheless, the battle was not to be easily won, though Polly did not nag her husband into changing his attitudes. Over a period of two years in this 'spiritual wilderness', she lovingly and prayerfully enticed her husband back to the place where he had been on fire for his Lord. It has been said in other places, and it was never more true than this, that behind every great man is a good woman. So it was that the day arrived when Smith Wigglesworth saw his need for restoration. At his own 'penitent form', in the privacy of his Victor Road home, he renewed his peace with God.

Recounting this part of his life some years later, Wigglesworth said, 'I can remember the time when I used to go white with rage, and shake all over with temper. I could hardly hold myself together. I waited on God for ten days. In those ten days I was being emptied out and the life of the Lord Jesus Christ was being wrought into me. My wife testified of the transformation that took place in my life. "I never saw such a change," said my wife. "I have never been able to cook anything since that time that has not pleased him. Nothing is too hot or too cold, everything is just right."'

The long road back to active faith

Wigglesworth had for a while abandoned his Christian faith. Some may ask if he needed to be 'saved' again. His views on this were expressed some time later. 'Once saved, always saved?' he was asked. Seeing he had a Salvation Army background, his reply was all the more interesting. 'You were saved by believing. Keep on believing and you will land.' Referring to Paul's words to the Christians in Rome, 'I appeal to you therefore, brethren, by the mercies of God, to present your bodies as a living sacrifice, holy and acceptable to God,' he said, 'It is not the end of sanctification – that has no end. It is not the end of the cleansing of the blood. It is wholly a life process – we are not saved twice, but we are out of fellowship many times.'

Hospitality became a prominent feature of their home. A trickle of visitors, frequently unexpected, soon became a stream. In fact, when special meetings had to be held in their Mission hall, Polly might even have described the number of visitors as a torrent. However, she took this in her stride along with her public ministry and supervision of their large house.

Smith Wigglesworth now returned to his ministry of personal witness with increased fervour. 'I was willing to wait an hour any day to have an interview with anyone about his soul's salvation,' he told his friend Stanley Frodsham. On one occasion when he was in the city centre he felt constrained to witness to someone about Jesus. So he asked God to direct him to the person of his choice. It was a very busy road and scores of people were passing every minute, but Wigglesworth wouldn't move until he felt the Spirit of God quickening him.

He was not blessed with a large supply of patience, and being a very busy businessman he became irritated by the delay of an hour and a half. So he somewhat impatiently prayed, 'Lord, I don't have much time to waste – please show me the man!' He was nothing if not blunt and many criticised him for this.

Soon after that prayer, he noticed a horse-drawn cart sandwiched between several other vehicles in the main thoroughfare. He knew the driver was his man. Undeterred by the heavy traffic and sidestepping like a light-footed rugby wing-half, he was quickly alongside the man and his cart. He leapt on to the moving cart and took his seat beside the driver. Without any of the niceties of an introduction, Smith launched into the plan of God's salvation for this man's life. 'Why don't you go about your own business? Why should you pick me out and talk to me?' growled the man. Smith wondered if he had made a mistake and silently said a prayer, 'Is this the right man, Lord?' Assured that this was the man, he continued to talk and plead with him to turn to Christ. The man started to cry, and Smith knew that God had softened the man's heart. Believing his work was done, Wigglesworth jumped from the cart and the man went on his way.

Three weeks later, Wigglesworth's mother told him this remarkable story. The previous evening she had been to the home of a man who was dying. He had been confined to his bed for three weeks. She asked the man if he would like someone to pray for him, and then he told her of a strange encounter he had with a man in the city centre. 'The last time I was out,' said the sick man, 'a young man got into my cart and spoke to me about Jesus. I was very rough with him but he was very persistent. Anyhow, God convicted me of my sins, and saved me.' The driver died that night.

The Public Executioner at the 'penitent form'

One of the hurdles confronting most Christian leaders today is the barrier between them and the man in the street. Wigglesworth was an earthy man, with hands soiled by hard work. He was a man's man. One day one of Bradford's vilest and most hated men came into his life, and as a result Wigglesworth's name is now preserved in Madame Tussaud's Chamber of Horrors in London. On Februrary 13th 1904, James Berry walked into one of the Wigglesworths' meetings; he was under deep conviction of sins and knelt beside Smith at the penitent form and surrendered his life to Christ.

Berry was the Crown's Public Executioner from 1884 to 1892. He was so vile and his language so filthy that even the most ungodly men of the city would avoid meeting him. He was responsible for all the executions in the area, and he later told Wigglesworth that he believed that the demon power in the murderers he hanged entered into him at their death. He was possessed with a legion of demons.

Although he had retired from the post of hangman some years earlier, the thoughts of the men he had executed haunted him day and night. In the end he determined to kill himself; he intended boarding a train in Bradford and hurling himself from it into the path of an oncoming train as a quick way of ending his miserable life. But God had other plans for him.

There was a young man at the railway depot who had been

converted at the Wigglesworths' Mission the previous evening. He was filled with newfound enthusiasm to witness to others about his saviour; seeing Berry standing alone at the station, he decided to witness him.

Eventually the young man persuaded the hangman to accompany him to the Mission for the evening service. There Berry experienced great conviction of sin. 'For two and a half hours', said Smith, 'he was literally sweating under conviction and you could see a vapour rising up from him.' Then he surrendered his life to God.

Wigglesworth sent up a silent prayer. 'Lord, tell me what to do.' He heard God tell him, 'Don't leave him. Go home with him.' Both men made their way to the new convert's home, where he said to his wife, 'God has saved me.' She was overwhelmed and wept many tears. Then she too gave her life to Christ. 'I tell you there was a difference in that home,' recalled Wigglesworth. 'Even the cat knew the difference.'

The sequel to that story is that James Berry, following his conversion, became a prominent campaigner for the abolition of the death penalty.

An example of faith-building

Wigglesworth's plumbing business continued to prosper. But he always had problems getting his customers to pay on time. 'I have always believed it was God's plan for me to be in need,' he would frequently assert. 'Because in the needy hour God would open the door for me and that strengthened my faith.' General William Booth, whom he continued to respect and admire, used to say, 'I always want my officers to keep in debt so that it will keep them on their knees.'

One day Wigglesworth was sorely in need of money to pay his men their wages, so he prayed. 'Lord, I have not time to go out and seek money. Please tell me where I can get some,' he asked. 'Go to Bishop,' he heard the Lord say to him. Unfortunately Bishop was notorious as a bad payer, and was frequently taken to court by his creditors. However, Smith had asked God for guidance and God had told him to go to Bishop. This was one of the faith-building steps in his early life. Later, when he was to challenge his hearers to have faith in God, it was against this kind of background, trusting God in all departments of life, that he was able to do so with confidence.

Kenneth Taylor's translation of Simon Peter's letter crystallises Smith Wigglesworth's experiences of these early days: 'These trials are only to test your faith, to see whether or not it is strong and pure. It is being tested as fire tests gold and purifies it – and your faith is far more precious to God than mere gold. So if your faith remains strong after being tried in the test tube of fiery trials, it will bring you much praise and glory and honour on the day of his return' (1 Peter 1:7, Living Bible).

After the answer to his prayer for guidance Wigglesworth mounted his faithful iron steed, his bicycle, and rode up to Bishop's mansion. When he arrived, the servant who answered the door told him that Bishop was away and would be for a further three weeks. 'That I cannot understand,' Smith said to the nonplussed servant. 'The Lord directed me to come here.' The servant hesitated, then asked Smith to wait. Within a short time she returned, and in her hand was the exact amount of money her employer owed. 'There,' she said, 'take it.' 'Do you do this often?' he enquired. 'No,' she replied, and then to Smith's amazement, she told him the following story. The previous evening, at about nine o'clock, she received her wages from her mistress, Bishop's wife. Even though she had never met or heard of Wigglesworth, she experienced an unaccountable urge to hold that money for someone she would meet shortly. This had happened at the same time as Wigglesworth heard God tell him to go to Bishop. 'What made you do it?' Smith asked the woman. 'I don't know,' she replied. 'All I can say is that I dare not let you go away without it.'

7 'I am the Lord that healeth thee'

Healing meetings in Leeds

Leeds was the north of England's main supply centre for the plumbing materials Wigglesworth used in his business. As it was only nine miles from Bradford, Smith went there every week. Now in his late twenties, Smith had been gloriously restored to the Lord. All his fire and zeal had returned and he took every opportunity to serve his master irrespective of the demands of his business. On one of his visits to Leeds he met a group of Christians who conducted divine healing meetings in the city. Smith was intrigued and each week he would meet with them. Turning the pages of his precious book the Bible, which, thanks to Polly, he was now able to read, they soon convinced him of the relevance of divine healing for the present day. He was impressed by the soundness of their doctrine, and eventually became convinced of its validity.

His weekly visits now took on a new dimension. Not only did he attend the healing services, he also took with him various sick people from Bradford. When he was unable to go he would still pay the travelling expenses of those too poor to pay for themselves. However, fearing that Polly would not approve, he kept these activities to himself, though not for long. In addition to her other capabilities, Polly was shrewd, and she soon discovered Smith's secret. To his astonishment however, she did not object; instead, she welcomed it. Furthermore, she went with him to one of the meetings and requested prayer for herself. Smith was overjoyed when Polly was immediately healed.

Coinciding with their introduction to divine healing during the latter part of the 1880s, the Wigglesworths were also enjoying increasing blessing on their own ministry. In the end they had to look for a larger hall, and eventually they moved to the now world-renowned hall in Bowland Street, Bradford, which they named 'The Bowland Street Mission'.

Wigglesworth continued to make weekly business trips to Leeds, but these were now combined with visits to the Leeds Healing Home, to which he continued to take the sick of Bradford. As he arrived at the Healing Home for one of his weekly visits, a leader remarked, 'Here's Wigglesworth bringing his sick friends from Bradford,' adding, 'If he only knew, these people could be healed in Bradford as easily as here in Leeds.'

Then an unusual set of circumstances began to occur. The Leeds meeting found itself without a suitable leader. The time for the Keswick Convention had come around and both the men responsible for the Leeds meetings wanted to attend the Keswick meetings. After discussing this between themselves, they decided to approach Wigglesworth to deputise for them and, hesitatingly, Smith agreed. At the first meeting he found himself confronted by fifteen people who had come forward for prayer. One was a Scotsman who hobbled forward on crutches. As soon as Wigglesworth prayed for him, he threw away his crutches and jumped around the room in great excitement. It was an electric moment for Smith. This was to be the beginning of Smith Wigglesworth's remarkable, even unique, ministry of healing.

Healings begin to happen in Bradford

With the events of the Leeds healing meetings to encourage him, Smith commenced similar meetings at his Bowland Street Mission. In one evening twelve people were miraculously healed. One person had a severe ulcer in the form of a discharging sore on her ankle joint. The next day it had completely disappeared except for a small scar where the ulcer had been.

Perhaps one of the most outstanding healings of these early days was that of a Bradford Baptist minister's wife.

It so happened that her husband needed to call at the Wigglesworths' house, and Smith could not help but notice how sad he looked. 'Anything wrong, Mr Clark?' enquired Wigglesworth. 'Yes,' he replied sadly. 'I have left my wife dying. Two doctors have been with her right through the night and they say she cannot live long.' 'Why don't you believe God for your wife?' Smith responded. 'I cannot,' said the man, somewhat hopelessly.

After Clark left, Wigglesworth could not get him out of his mind. Eventually he could endure it no longer: he went to see a Christian leader who believed in divine healing and lived nearby. He told the man of his encounter with the Baptist minister and asked if he would accompany him to the manse so that they both could pray for the woman. Surprisingly the man refused. Then he said to Wigglesworth, 'I believe if you will go, God will heal.' Encouraged by this, Smith made his way to the woman's home.

At this time Smith was young and inexperienced and still feeling the need for support, so on the way he called on another man, named Nichols. Nichols was a devout man, but, 'if he got the opportunity to pray, would pray all around the world three times and then come back'. Nichols agreed to accompany him.

On their arrival in the bedroom, Wigglesworth invited Nichols to pray and not stop until he, Wigglesworth, had completed his ministry to the dying lady. It seemed a golden opportunity for Nichols to pray at great length, so with much delight he embarked on his marathon prayer.

Wigglesworth was soon to regret his invitation. Recounting this story some time later, he said, 'I have never ever suffered so much as I did that day when he was praying.' Nichols prayed for the husband who was going to be bereaved and for the children who would be left motherless. 'He piled it on so thick that I had to cry out, "Stop him. Please Lord, stop this man praying."' So the man stopped. Smith then asked the husband to pray. And the same mournful prayer followed. Again, now in extreme desperation, he cried out, 'Lord stop him.' He too stopped.

Now Wigglesworth knew the verses of James 4 about anointing people with oil before you pray for their healing, but he didn't know how much he should use. He had come fully prepared with a half-pint bottle of oil in his pocket and realising that it would be better if he prayed for the woman himself, he launched into his prayer as soon as the husband stopped. Then, as he prayed, he took the bottle from his pocket, unscrewed the stopper, and poured the entire contents over the dying woman's head.

The oil cascaded over the semiconscious woman, spilling all over the bed. 'I was a novice at the time,' said Wigglesworth, 'and I did not know any better.' But his prayer was answered in a most dramatic manner. The effect was as sensational to Wigglesworth as it was to Mrs Clark. This is how he described it: 'I was standing beside her at the top of her bed looking towards the foot when suddenly the Lord Jesus appeared. I had my eyes open gazing on him. There he was at the foot of the bed. He gave me one of those gentle smiles. After a few moments he vanished. But something that day happened that changed the whole of my life.' It also changed the whole Clark household. Mrs Clark was completely healed and lived to raise a family of several children, outliving her husband by several years.

'Physician, heal yourself'

Smith Wigglesworth was also a sick man. Though a strong advocate of divine healing for others, he continued to suffer from haemorrhoids, a sickness that had been with him since childhood.

Once again Polly was to play a significant role in setting the course for Smith's unique future ministry. Very gently but adroitly, when she and Smith were in conversation with a

visiting preacher, she asked the visitor, who was also engaged
in the ministry of healing, what he would say to a man who
prayed for others to be healed but used medication for his
own sickness. Without hesitation, he said, 'I would say that
the man did not fully trust the Lord.'

The answer hit Wigglesworth hard, and stung him into
action. When the meal had finished and Smith and the
visiting preacher were alone, Smith confessed, 'When my wife
was talking about one who preached divine healing to others
and yet used other means himself, she was referring to me.
From childhood I have suffered from haemorrhoids or piles
and so I deem it necessary to use salts every day. I have looked
upon them as harmless, natural means. I knew that if I did not
have something of this kind, I should have bleeding every
day, and infection might result. But if you will stand with me
in faith, I am willing to trust God in this matter and give up
the salts. Since I have taken them every day for years, my
system is so used to them that there will be no natural
function from now until Wednesday. Will you stand with me
in faith on that day? For in the natural I shall have great pain
and much bleeding through not having used the salts.'
Without further ado, both these men entered into a pact to
trust God for Smith's complete healing.

Following that incident on the Sunday, Wigglesworth
refrained from taking his daily dose of salts. When the
following Wednesday arrived and he knew it would be the
critical moment, he annointed himself with oil. Recounting
that event, he would testify, 'God undertook. My bowels
functioned that day like a baby's. God had perfectly healed
me.'

His faith was one of complete simplicity. 'Does divine
healing embrace seasickness?' he was once asked. 'Yes,'
Wigglesworth replied. 'It is a spirit of fear that causes your
seasickness, and I command that spirit to go out of you in
Jesus' name.' In all his future travels that man was never
seasick again.

One other experience of personal healing must be included.

He was at the Bowland Street Mission Hall one Sunday when he was gripped by a violent pain in his abdomen. Two men came to his rescue and supported him as he collapsed in agony. Prayer was offered for him throughout the night but it appeared to be of no avail. Instead he grew worse. In the morning he said to Polly, 'It seems to me that this is my home-call. It does not seem as though anything can be done. You know our arrangement is that when we know we have received a home-call, only then, to save each other the embarrassment of having an inquest and the condemnation of outsiders, would we call a doctor. To protect yourself you should now call a physician.'

Deeply distressed, but recognising the wisdom of Smith's advice, she called a doctor. The doctor's prognosis was, 'There is no hope whatever.' Smith had been suffering from appendicitis for the previous six months and the only course open now was for an immediate operation. But because of his weakened condition it was doubtful whether an operation could be performed. The doctor left promising to return later in the day after fulfilling other urgent calls.

Soon after the doctor departed an elderly lady accompanied by a young man arrived. In Wigglesworth's words, 'She was a great woman to pray, and she believed that everything that was not healed was of the devil.' The woman began to pray and, as she did so, the young man laid his hands on Wigglesworth and cried out, 'Come out devil, in the name of Jesus.'

Here Wigglesworth takes up the story. 'To my surprise I felt as well as I had ever been in my life. I was absolutely free from pain. As soon as they had prayed for me they went downstairs, and I got up, believing that no one had a right to remain in bed when healed. When I got downstairs, my wife cried, "Oh!" I said, "I am healed." She said, "I hope it is true." I inquired, "Any work in?" "Yes," she replied.' Taking the address where the work was to be done, Smith left the house.

Soon afterwards, and when Wigglesworth was still out working, the doctor returned. Placing his silk hat on the table

in the hall, he began to walk up the stairs to the bedroom.
'Doctor, doctor,' Polly called. 'He's out. He's gone to work.'
The astonished doctor shook his head saying, 'They'll bring
him back a corpse, as sure as you live.'

When telling this story later in life, Wigglesworth said, 'I
have laid hands on people with appendicitis in almost every
part of the world and never knew of a case not instantly
healed, even when doctors were on the premises.'

Following that experience Smith and Polly sat across the
table in their home and looking into each other's face made
this solemn pledge: 'From henceforth no medicine, no
doctors, no drugs of any kind shall come into our house.'
Even so, he neither despised nor condemned others who used
medication for their illnesses. His decision, he would say, was
very personal – it was something between God and him and
not to be imposed on others. For him to engage in the type of
ministry he exercised, and the like of which is hard to find in
another man, he had to do this in his own way.

Answers to questions

Perhaps I should here consider the question that may have
arisen in the minds of some readers: How could Wigglesworth exercise one of the gifts of the Holy Spirit before he
had been 'baptised in the Spirit'? (For an explanation of the
term 'baptism' from a Pentecostal point of view, please turn
to Appendix 1 at the end of this book.)

It was a question asked of Wigglesworth some years later
when he was preaching in an Assemblies of God church in
San Francisco: 'Are the results mentioned in Mark chapter 16
verses 16 to 18, to apply only to those who are baptised with
the Holy Spirit?' Wigglesworth replied: 'Thousands of people
who have never received the baptism of the Holy Spirit are
very specially led and blessed in healing the sick. The finest
people that ever I did know, who have never come into the
same experience as I am in today regarding the baptism of the

Holy Spirit, are mightily used with all kinds of sicknesses wonderfully. But they did not have that which is in the 16th chapter of Mark. Only baptised believers speak in tongues. "If you believe, you shall lay hands on the sick, and if you believe, you shall speak in new tongues" – meaning to say, after the Holy Spirit is come, you are in the place of command. You can command. How do I know it? Because Paul in 2 Timothy chapter 2 is very clear when he says, "Stir up the gift". What was the trouble with Timothy? He was downcast. He was a young man, called out by Paul, and had been amongst the presbytery. And because of his youth he had been somewhat put to one side, and he was grieved. Paul found him in a distressed place, so Paul stirred him up.

'Everyone of you, if you had faith, can stir up the gift within you. The Holy Spirit can be so manifest in you that you can speak – it may not be in gift, but speak in utterances by tongues. And I believe everybody baptised in the Holy Spirit to have perfect control and speak every day, morning, noon and night in this order.

'Do not put out your hand to stop anybody that is doing good, but encourage them to do good, then bring them into the "baptism of much good".'

To many his answer will appear unsatisfactory. If one gift may be exercised before a person is baptised in the Spirit, why not all? In this promise of Christ the gift of tongues is included with that of healing.

Later in this book you will read some of Wigglesworth's teaching on the gifts of the Holy Spirit. For example, when giving a Bible study on the 'Gifts of Healing' he said in his introduction: 'The Holy Spirit people have a ministry. All the people who have received the Holy Spirit might be so filled with the Holy Spirit that without having the gift, the Holy Spirit within them brings forth healing power. That is the reason why I say to you people – never be afraid of coming near me when I am praying for the sick. I love to have people to help me. Why? Because I know there are people in this place who have a very dim conception of what they have got. I believe the power of the Holy Spirit which you have received has power so to bring you into concentration that you dare believe for God to heal apart from knowing you have a gift.'

Smith and Polly Wigglesworth, as a testimony to the Lord's healing power in their newly acquired Bowland Street Mission, arranged for a very large scroll to be painted on the wall facing the congregation. On the scroll were the words, 'I am the Lord that healeth thee.'

8 'Bring me higher up the mountain'

Holiness and the 'second blessing'

Bring me higher up the mountain
Into fellowship with Thee
In Thy light I see the fountain
And the Blood that cleanses me

This hymn of aspiration was sung weekly, sometimes daily, during the first period of my theological schooling during the late 1930s. It was also the time when I was present at some of Smith Wigglesworth's meetings. Now as I read again his sermons I am reminded of those days and the words of this hymn. They bring back to me the least acknowledged part of his life: holiness.

Mention Wigglesworth's name and two words spring to the minds of most people who have heard of him: faith and healing. But he was also greatly influenced in his early Christian life by Bible teachers of sanctification and holiness at the annual Keswick conventions. Smith and Polly Wigglesworth were frequent visitors to Keswick. In those days emphasis on the teaching of a second work of grace as the 'second blessing' (sometimes described as 'baptism in the Holy Spirit', but not to be confused with the Pentecostal teaching on this experience), was common in these convention meetings.

This is how Smith Wigglesworth described what he believed at that time: 'My wife and I always believed in scriptural holiness, but I was conscious of much carnality in myself. A really holy man once came to preach for us and he spoke of what it means to be entirely sanctified. He called it a very definite work of grace subsequent to the new birth. As I waited on the Lord for ten days in prayer, handing my body over to him as a living sacrifice according to Romans chapter 12 and verses 1 and 2, God surely did something for me ... We counted that as the baptism in the Spirit. And so, at our Bowland Street Mission we stood for both healing and holiness.'

Later we will look at Smith's 'Pentecostal baptism', but in his thinking it was always associated with holiness. There are Pentecostal teachers who teach that this baptism is for power and not holiness, but Wigglesworth would have none of that. 'The Holy Spirit will come when a man is cleansed,' were his words, adding, 'there must be a purging of the old life. I never saw anyone baptised who was not clean within.'

When giving a series of Bible studies on the subject, he referred to a man who sought the 'baptism' at one of his meetings. The man was very restless. When questioned by Wigglesworth, he replied that God was revealing things to him about his life which made him feel unworthy. 'Repent of everything that is wrong,' counselled Smith. The man continued his times of waiting for the fullness of the Spirit, but without success.

'These times of waiting on God for the fullness of the Spirit are times when he searches the heart and tries the reins,' Wigglesworth told him. 'Tell the Lord you will do it [put right the wrong you have done in your business], and never mind the consequences.' The man paid the account that no one knew he owed, and Wigglesworth prayed for him and he was baptised in the Spirit immediately. 'They that bear the vessels of the Lord must be clean, must be holy.'

The possibility of further spiritual blessing

Smith Wigglesworth was now forty-eight. He was a very successful businessman, and his spiritual life was healthy.

Bowland Street Mission was thriving, many people were being blessed and it was gaining a reputation for its emphasis on the teaching of holiness and healing. 'We thought that we had got all that was coming to us on spiritual lines,' he said. However, he continued to be limited in his public ministry. He still found great difficulty in stringing even a few words together let alone sentences. Polly was always the preacher, though she repeatedly encouraged Smith to share the preaching with her. She would often announce that on the following Sunday her husband would preach the sermon, but such events were invariably accompanied by agonising days for Smith. Then the 'sermons' would be short-lived and end by Wigglesworth inviting members of the congregation to the pulpit to finish the preaching.

One day Smith heard of unusual happenings in an Anglican church in Sunderland. From all accounts, Christians were receiving similar experience to the early church as recorded in the Acts of the Apostles. 'Have you heard the latest?' said a visitor to his home. 'They are receiving the Holy Spirit in Sunderland and speaking in tongues. I have decided to go and see this thing for myself,' continued the man. 'Would you like to come with me?' And the man offered to pay Smith's travelling expenses.

9   The significance of Sunderland

The background to the Pentecostal movement

Some six thousand miles away, on the west coast of North America, a remarkable spiritual awakening had occurred in a derelict building, a wooden barn-like structure, in Azusa Street in Los Angeles. It had been converted into a meeting place for some Christians under the leadership of a humble black preacher by the name of W J Seymour. On April 9th 1906 the 'fire fell' as on the day of Pentecost in Jerusalem in AD 33, and those Californian Christians were caught up into the seventh heaven, were overwhelmed by the power of the Holy Spirit and spoke in 'other tongues' as the Spirit gave them utterance.

In June the same year, Rachel Sizelone and her husband were attending a Free Methodist Church Camp meeting nearby. On his way to one of the meetings her husband happened to pass by this old building, and 'heard wonderful singing in the Spirit'. He shared this with his wife Rachel and, filled with curiosity, they both ventured into one of these meetings.

They were immediately impressed by the presence of God in this humble place 'with its low ceilings and rough floor' where 'cobwebs were hanging in the windows and joists'. This was in direct contrast to the elegant churches with which they were more familiar. (However, 'the building was soon cleaned out, and the ceilings were whitewashed'.)

'A large box served as the pulpit,' said Mrs Sizelone. 'William J Seymour (a black minister) stayed behind the box on his knees before the Lord.' (This was a ministry he had in common with Evan Roberts in the Welsh Revival of 1904 –

maybe news of the blessing in Wales had also reached him.)
Rachel Sizelone continued, 'My soul cried out, "O Lord,
these people have something I do not have."' She then
listened carefully as Seymour 'gave out the Word' and she
said to herself, 'Well, praise God, he is not doing away with
any of my experiences or beliefs, but just adding to my
experience – the baptism in the Holy Spirit, which he
[Seymour] said could come only to a clean heart.'

At the same time in Oslo, Norway, a young Methodist
minister was thinking of ways by which he could raise money
for his church building, unaware of the 'happenings' in
Azusa Street. He decided to appeal to the American
churches for help. So it was that in the autumn of 1906 the
Rev T B Barratt found himself in New York.

As Barratt made enquiries about suitable churches where
he could expect a favourable response to his appeal, he
encountered some 'young Pentecostalists' (young, that is, in
experience). Their exuberance and enthusiasm for the things
of God took a hold on this man. It was October 7th 1906, a
day he would never forget, a day that blotted out his
financial needs, a day that was to change his life and his
church in Norway and a day that was to disturb the still
waters of Britain's churches and send ripples circling
throughout Europe and the British Empire. 'I was filled with
light and such power that I began to shout as loud as I could
in a foreign language. I must have spoken seven or eight
languages to judge from the various sounds and forms of
speech used. I stood erect at times, preaching in one foreign
tongue after another, and I know from the strength of my
voice that ten thousand might easily have heard all I said.
The most wonderful moment was when I burst into a
beautiful baritone solo, using one of the most pure and
delightful languages I have ever heard. The tune and the
words were entirely new to me and the rhythm and cadence
of the various choruses seemed to be perfect.'

This description from any man would be impressive, but it
comes with greater weight when you know that the man was

a student of the renowned Norwegian musician and composer, Grieg. Barratt was an accomplished musician and soloist.

Thomas Bell Barratt, an Englishman by birth, returned to Norway on December 9th and immediately introduced his congregation to his new-found spiritual experience. Pentecostal fires rapidly spread throughout Scandinavia.

Two years earlier revival fires had raged through the valleys of South Wales under the leadership of Evan Roberts. Reports of these events had reached a small Anglican parish church in Monkwearmouth, part of the borough of Sunderland, an English seaport and industrial town on the northeast coast. The vicar of that parish was a godly man named Alexander Boddy.

The late Donald Gee in his history of the *The Pentecostal Movement* wrote, 'It is impossible, and would be historically incorrect, to dissociate the Pentecostal Movement from the remarkable visitation of God's Spirit [on the occasion of the Welsh Revival of 1904]. The profound impression which the Welsh Revival made upon the Christian world can scarcely be realised by those who were not living at the time. Visitors came from far and near. Newspapers sent special reporters, and published lengthy reports ... It seemed, for the time, like an irresistible torrent.

'Perhaps the most formative result was the creation of a widespread spirit of expectation for still greater things. Men justly asked "Why Wales only?" Why not other lands? Why not a world-wide revival? Prayer to that end received a tremendous new impetus ... Of special interest to British people is the little group that gathered around the godly vicar of All Saints' Parish Church, Sunderland. Alexander Boddy had been their spiritual leader since 1886. When the revival broke out in Wales in 1904 he made a special journey to Wales and stood beside Evan Roberts in the midst of some of the amazing scenes of Tonypandy. When he recounted to his people at All Saints' what he had personally seen in Wales it stirred both pastor and people up to yet more earnest prayer and expectation of great things from God. Sunderland was being prepared in the purposes of God to become a centre of new and far-reaching blessing.'

Boddy and a small group of his parishioners continued earnestly in prayer for an outpouring of the Holy Spirit on his congregation for another two years, and then he heard of the blessings in Oslo under the ministry of Barratt, recently returned from USA. Once again Alexander Boddy travelled in search of accurate information. Early in 1907 he was in Norway, this time alongside the Methodist minister T B Barratt, witnessing the revival that was taking place.

Returning home he wrote, 'My four days in Christiania [as it was then known – it is now Oslo] can never be forgotten. I stood with Evan Roberts in Tonypandy, but have never witnessed such scenes as those in Norway.' Later that year Boddy published a pamphlet entitled *Pentecostal for England* which he distributed at the Keswick Convention of 1907. In the pamphlet he wrote, 'It is said that 20,000 people today are speaking in tongues, or have so spoken.'

Barratt decided to return to the United States to renew his contacts with the men and women who were now emerging as leaders of the young Pentecostal movement. Hearing of his intentions, Boddy persuaded him to call at Sunderland en route. And so it was that this Norwegian Methodist minister, a forerunner of the Pentecostal movement in Europe, found himself in an Anglican pulpit in September 1907 describing the baptism of the Holy Spirit with the speaking in other tongues. (This would have been unthinkable even thirty years ago, let alone eighty years ago.)

At the prayer meeting following that Sunday evening service a few of those present experienced an astonishing phenomenon. The meeting continued until four o'clock on Monday morning. The effect was dramatic. It revolutionised All Saints' Parish Church and, though the vicar and his parishioners did not realise it at the time, it was to mark the beginning of the British Pentecostal movement. It was not Alexander Boddy's intention to break from the Church of

England, but subsequent events, such as the disapproval of the Anglican and Free Church hierarchy, forced these and other Christians out of their existing religious denominations. Nevertheless it must be recorded that the wise and saintly Bishop Handley G Moule, who was Bishop of Durham at this time, though not a participant in these events, did not raise any ecclesiastical hindrances.

Before this separation took place, something else happened which must have impressed the church authorities even if they disapproved of these strange events: there was an outstanding demonstration of love and generosity by the congregation. One of the side effects was that the church debt was immediately cleared. To this day a plaque to commemorate this can be seen on the parish church hall; it reads:

September 1907
When the fire of the Lord fell
it burned up the debt

Four days that changed a life

Smith Wigglesworth was not aware of these remarkable developments as he boarded the train for Sunderland. His Bowland Street Mission was experiencing spiritual blessings more than neighbouring churches. Many healings were taking place through his ministry. There was more power in his personal evangelism. However, although he reckoned that he had been baptised in the Holy Spirit (as taught at the Keswick Convention meetings), he was not fully satisfied, and when on the platform in his Mission hall he continued to be tongue-tied, leaving Polly to do the preaching. But now that the news of people speaking in tongues in Sunderland – just as they did in the beginning of Christianity – had been given to him, he could not rest until he knew all about it for himself.

On his arrival, he was met by two former members of his Bradford Mission, now living in Sunderland. They did not lose time in warning him against the meetings at All Saints'. They believed them to be heretical and contrary to the scriptures. Undeterred by this, Smith and his travelling companion decided to attend Mr Boddy's prayer meeting without delay. And so it was that on Saturday October 25th, just a month after the visit of T B Barratt, Wigglesworth found himself in the parish hall of All Saints' Church, Monkwearmouth.

God's blessing was already being experienced in Bradford, and the night before Wigglesworth had left for Sunderland many people had fallen prostrate on the floor under the power of God. In contrast, the All Saints' meeting was 'flat'. He began to wonder why he had come; there did not seem to be as much power as in his Bowland Street Mission. He was disappointed. 'But I was hungry for God,' said Smith. And he knew that God was aware of his hunger however much he was to be misunderstood by the others at the 'waiting meetings'.

A feature of these early Pentecostal meetings was 'testimony time', similar to the Methodist class meetings of Smith's youth. One man who made an impression on Wigglesworth testified to having spoken in tongues after waiting on God for three weeks. Not given to the niceties of behaviour, Smith called out, 'Let's hear those tongues. That's what I came for. Let's hear it.' 'When you are baptised in the Spirit you will speak in tongues,' he was told.

Smith Wigglesworth was throughout his whole life nothing if not earnest. He sought more and more of God with his whole heart. So it was that at seven o'clock the next morning, Sunday October 26th, he went to the Salvation Army prayer meeting. 'Three times in that prayer meeting I was smitten to the floor by the mighty power of God,' he said. 'Somewhat ashamed of my position, lest I should be misunderstood, I tried to control myself by sitting up again and kneeling and praying.' Wigglesworth had an experience that morning similar to the one described by Daniel 10; he 'continued with the Holy Spirit glow all the day still realising a mightier work to follow'.

Later that day, now at All Saints', he attended Holy

Communion followed by the 'waiting meetings' which were arranged for those seeking the Pentecostal baptism. His hunger for God continued to increase and he continued in prayer throughout Monday October 27th. At about eleven o'clock on the Tuesday morning October 28th, he was on his knees in the vicarage when 'the fire fell and burned in me until the Holy Spirit revealed absolute purity before God . . . My whole being became full of light and holy presence, and in the revelation I saw an empty cross. At the same time I could see the Jesus I loved and adored, crowned in the Glory in a reigning position.'

For four days Smith had wanted nothing but God. But he now began to feel the pressure of his business back home. With some reluctance he came to the decision that he had to return home even though he had not received the Pentecostal baptism and spoken in tongues.

He told Mrs Boddy, the vicar's wife, of his decision, concluding, 'I'm going away, but I've not received the tongues yet.' 'It's not tongues you need,' replied the woman wisely, 'it's the baptism.' He protested that he had already received his baptism some years before, in July 1893 to be precise. Then, as he was about to leave, he added that he would still be glad to have her lay hands on him.

This gracious and godly lady agreed to pray for him there in the vicarage. As she did so he felt the fire-power of the Holy Spirit lay hold of him as never before. Mrs Boddy left the room and Wigglesworth remained alone, 'bathed in the power of God'. 'I was conscious of the cleansing of the precious blood and I cried out in a new-found ecstasy, "Clean! Clean! Clean!"' He was filled with an increased consciousness of cleansing. Then he began to speak in languages unknown to him. His whole being was enveloped with an unusual feeling as waves of worship began to roll over him. So intense was the sense of God's presence that he remained there, unable to move, praising and glorifying his saviour for a long time. 'I began to praise him in other tongues as the Spirit gave me utterance,' he later told his wife.

'I could no longer speak in English. Then I knew that though I had previously received anointings, now I had received the baptism in the Holy Spirit as they did on the day of Pentecost.'

When recalling these events he would say, 'Today I am actually living in the Acts of the Apostles' time,' with the qualification that, 'The moment you pass through the Acts of the Apostles you are ready for the Epistles. The Epistles are written for baptised believers.'

Wigglesworth was always a blunt Yorkshiremañ who said what he thought without fear of the consequences. Many thought him uncouth and resented his brusqueness. Nevertheless he was sincere and honest and always avoided sham and hypocrisy. Immediately after his baptism he returned to the meeting which was then in progress and interrupted the vicar who was on his feet speaking. Smith asked if he could speak. Alexander Boddy agreed to this unusual request, promptly took his seat and allowed Wigglesworth to address the meeting.

The effect was dramatic. Though previously he had never been able to hold the attention of any congregation for the briefest of periods, now those in the meeting gave him rapt attention as he spoke with great conviction. When he had finished, a man stood to his feet and said, 'We have been rebuking this man because he was so intensely hungry, but he has come to us for a few days and has received the baptism. And some of us have been waiting here for weeks and have not received.' This stirred the congregation to the extent that within a short time fifty of those present were filled with the Holy Spirit and spoke in other tongues.

Doubts defeated and a challenge issued

Smith Wigglesworth's next move was equally dramatic. He sent a telegram to Polly which said, 'I have received the baptism in the Holy Ghost and have spoken in tongues.' But during the train journey home the devil began to torment him, 'Are you going to take this thing to Bradford?' The way he felt just at that moment was that he had nothing to take, and he began to question the rashness of sending the telegram to his wife.

However, he soon checked himself. He had always said that you should rely on your faith in God and not your own feelings. So, in his customary if somewhat unique style, and to the astonishment of his fellow travellers in the railway coach, he shouted aloud, 'Yes, I'm taking it!'

His son George was waiting for him when he arrived at Bradford's railway station. 'Father, have you been speaking in tongues?' 'Yes, George,' replied Wigglesworth. 'Then let's hear you,' said George. But Smith said nothing; he did not even try. He was always strongly opposed to invitations to speak in tongues as a demonstration, and later condemned such practices as 'activities of the "flesh"'.

Father and son made their way home to find mother waiting for them. Polly could be as direct with her words as Smith. As he stepped inside their home she looked him up and down with a calculated gaze. 'So you've been speaking in tongues, have you?' she said somewhat scornfully. In a subdued voice he responded, 'Well, er . . . yes.' 'Well, I want you to understand,' said his wife rather firmly, 'I am as much baptised as you are, and I don't speak in tongues.' Then pushing the knife in a little further, she added, 'I've been preaching for more than twenty years and you have sat beside me on the platform tongue-tied. But on Sunday you'll preach yourself my man, and I'll be there to see what there is in it.' That said, she walked out of the room, leaving a very thoughtful, and perhaps a little shaken, Smith Wigglesworth.

'What's happened to the man?'

Polly Wigglesworth kept her word. On the following Sunday she took her seat on one of the long benches at the back of the mission hall alongside a young woman, called Florence Teear, who was to become Polly's daughter-in-law, the wife of Seth and mother of Leslie. 'It was a remarkable event. Father Wigglesworth was always neatly and cleanly dressed. He used to sit on the platform but never preach,' she told me in her Lancashire home near the Irish Sea not long before she died.

Smith walked the length of the hall and, with a small Bible in his hand, ascended the three short steps to the platform. As he walked towards the front of the hall he did not know what he was going to say in his sermon. But as he ascended the platform steps God spoke to him. He was told to begin with the words in Isaiah 61: 'The Spirit of the Lord God is upon me, because the Lord has anointed me to bring good tidings to the afflicted; he has sent me to bind up the brokenhearted, to proclaim liberty to the captives, and the opening of the prison to those who are bound.'

Then he began to preach. Soon he felt the mighty power of God surge through him, and though he had a limited vocabulary, words rushed out of him like a torrent of water. Previously when he had attempted to preach he had always broken down weeping, but now he was fluent. Furthermore, he marched around the platform, fully at ease like a seasoned speaker.

Polly sat at the back of the hall. She was completely astounded and could hardly believe her ears, let alone her eyes. She could not keep still. As Smith continued with his preaching so Polly kept moving, from one part of the bench to another, and then another, talking to herself. 'That's not my Smith. That's not my Smith.' Then she would add, 'Amazing, amazing,' and 'What's happened to the man?' And that's how she continued throughout his sermon, unable to keep still and sitting on every part of that long bench at the back of Bowland Street Mission hall. Florence Wigglesworth chuckled as she told me the story.

Polly watched this uneducated and previously fumbling, stumbling plumber of the Yorkshire Dales, her much loved

Smith, speaking not only coherently but with a force that would have been the envy of many a politician. Later he said, 'Suddenly I felt that I had prophetic utterances which were flowing like a river by the power of the Holy Spirit.'

As Smith Wigglesworth stood to announce the closing hymn the secretary of the mission rose to his feet and said to the congregation, 'I want what our leader has received.' But as he went to sit down he missed his seat and fell lengthwise on the floor. Then Seth Wigglesworth, Smith's eldest son, stood up and said that he also wanted what his father had experienced, but when he tried to sit down he missed his seat and he too went sprawling along the floor. A further eleven members of that congregation did the same. 'The strangest thing', recounted Wigglesworth, 'was that they were all laughing in the Spirit, and laughing at each other. The Lord had really turned again this captivity of Zion, and the mouths of his children were being filled with laughter according to the Word of the Lord in Psalm 126.'

That was the beginning of the Pentecostal movement in Bradford, with many hundreds receiving the baptism in the Holy Spirit accompanied by the gift of tongues.

10 They called it the 'tongues movement'

The Pentecostal movement was soon labelled by its critics and opponents as 'the tongues movement' (see Appendix 1). It has to be said here, that although Wigglesworth and his contemporaries placed emphasis on the use of 'tongues', more was made of it by their critics than they did themselves. It was used as a derisory term. The light, love, laughter and power that accompanied these spiritual manifestations were either not recognised or they were deliberately ignored.

Admittedly, speaking in tongues is a strange phenomenon, but the scriptural record clearly states that the early Christians practised this not only in Jerusalem at the festival of Pentecost but also in other countries surrounding the Mediterranean Sea.

Smith Wigglesworth's understanding of tongues

Wigglesworth held the view, now discarded by most Pentecostal teachers, that there is a difference between the act of speaking in tongues on the occasion of being baptised in the Holy Spirit and the gift of tongues as listed in 1 Corinthians 12. He also took the then commonly held but now largely discarded view that the Spirit of Christ is different from the Holy Spirit. However, he repeatedly rebuked those of his congregation who caused disturbances by speaking in tongues when he thought they were out of order. On one occasion he shouted to a man in one of his meetings who interrupted his preaching with a 'message in tongues'. He thundered out from the pulpit in his broad

Yorkshire accent, 'Shut up man. Don't you dare interrupt God's message through me. Sit down.' The man sat down, and shut up.

Wigglesworth was quick to defend his experience of speaking in tongues in the vicarage in Sunderland as evidence of his baptism in the Holy Spirit, although he also testified to outstanding 'anointings' of the Holy Spirit in meetings he attended in Methodism, the Salvation Army and at Keswick. In one of his studies on this subject he had this to say. 'There are two sides to this baptism: the first is, you possess the Spirit; the second is that the Spirit possesses you. The first has to be, before the second can be. This is my message at this time – being possessed by the Baptiser, and not merely possessing the Baptiser. There is no limit to the possibilities of such a life, because it has God behind it, in the midst of it, and through it. I see people from time to time very slack, cold and indifferent. But after they get filled with the Holy Spirit they become ablaze for God. I believe that God's ministers are to be flames of fire. Nothing less than flames. Nothing less than mighty instruments with burning messages, with hearts full of love. They must have a depth of consecration that God has taken full charge of the body and it exists only that it may manifest the glory of God.'

Speaking to the Christians in Pudsey, Yorkshire, many years after his Sunderland experience, he likened it to a baptism into death in which the person is purified and energised, bringing the soul 'where it touches ideal immensity'. He was repeatedly to emphasise the inner experience as superior to the outward expression.

'Don't be afraid when people are on the floor. Lots of people roll about the floor and get their black clothes made white. Any number of things take place when the flesh is giving way to the Spirit. But after the Holy Spirit has come in, then we do not expect you to roll again on the floor. We only expect you to roll on the floor until the life of the personality of the Holy Spirit has got right in, turned you out, and you will be able to stand up and preach then, instead of rolling on the floor!

'There are some people who are so full of the Holy Spirit that they feel inwardly moved and sometimes their whole body moves. When you are full of the Holy Spirit you may be moved in your body, and many things happen. But it is not the best. The best is that the gifts are manifested, and then the other subsides. Everybody who is filled with the Holy Spirit, we are glad for them to have great joy and many things. But we want you to excel to the edifying of the church.'

Spiritual hunger

The secret of spiritual success is a hunger that persists. To Wigglesworth the worst that can come to any child of God is to be satisfied with his present spiritual attainments. 'It is an awful condition,' he would tell his hearers. God, he believed, was and is looking for hungry, thirsty people. And that is how Wigglesworth received his baptism.

During a visit to the Elim Pentecostal Church in Clapham, London, he told how he was given hospitality by a certain church. His host for the occasion had been shopping prior to the meeting, so he was laden with many parcels as Wigglesworth accompanied him on the walk to his home. As they were passing the first lamppost on their route, Smith said to his host, 'Brother, are you baptised in the Holy Spirit?' 'No,' replied the man. 'Then you will be tonight,' said Wigglesworth. As they walked on he repeated the question. At every lamppost they passed he would ask the same question. There were about a hundred lampposts en route. Everytime the man said 'No' Wigglesworth, with monotonous regularity, would then challenge him, 'Say you will be tonight.' By the time they reached his home the man was beginning to wish he hadn't agreed to having Wigglesworth as his overnight guest. Eventually they arrived at the garden gate. As they did so, and to the man's complete astonishment, the agile Smith leapt over the wall and faced his host from the other side of the gate. 'Now,' he said to the by now somewhat frightened brother, 'you don't come in here unless you say

you will be baptised in the Holy Spirit tonight.' 'Oh, I do feel
so funny,' said the man, 'but I will say it.' Thereupon Smith
opened the gate and followed the man into the house. As soon
as they entered he was introduced to the wife. Without
waiting to be seated Wigglesworth barked at the woman, 'Are
you baptised in the Holy Spirit?' In astonishment at this blunt
approach from a stranger, she stammered 'N-n-o', but added,
with some trepidation, 'But I want to be.' 'You and your
husband will be,' he assured her, 'and before we go to bed
tonight.'

The supper was on the table and, aware that he would not
have eaten for several hours because of his travels, she invited
him to take his seat without further delay. But Smith would
have none of that. 'First things first' was his motto. He told
the couple, 'No supper for anyone until you are both baptised
in the Holy Spirit.'

When he told the story someone called out, 'Were they
baptised?' 'Oh yes,' responded Wigglesworth. 'They were
soon speaking in tongues.' Wigglesworth repeatedly said, 'If
you leave people as you found them, God is not speaking by
you. If you are not making people mad or glad, there is
something amiss with your ministry. If there is not a war on,
it's a bad job for you.'

Another contemporary of Wigglesworth was a lawyer
named T H Mundell who was the godson of Dr Tait, one-
time Archbishop of Canterbury. He received his baptism in
his own home at six o'clock in the morning one September
day in 1908. This is how he described his experience: 'I awoke
full of joy and praise. I lifted up both my arms in the dark,
praising Jesus aloud, full of joy and peace. And whilst I was
doing so the whole room seemed to be filled with the very
presence of God . . . I immediately got down on my knees at
my bedside to worship God and thank Him. In trying to
praise Him I could no longer speak in my own language, but a
volume poured from my heart in adoration and praise to God
in various languages. And I seemed unable to speak in my
own language.'

Wigglesworth again: 'I believe it is wrong to wait for the Holy Spirit – the Holy Spirit is waiting for us.'

11   Ever-widening circles

Smith's ministry extends

Earlier I likened the spread of the Pentecostal movement to ripples from centres of the Spirit's outpouring – Los Angeles, Oslo, Stockholm, Sunderland, to name the early few. The ministry of Smith Wigglesworth extended in like manner. Following his Pentecostal experience he was inundated with preaching invitations.

The first one of significance came from a Lancashire man who had a factory that employed a thousand workers. 'If you'll come,' wrote the owner, 'I'll close my factory for the afternoon of each day, and give you five meetings between 1 pm and 11 pm.' He received a reply which, in typical Wigglesworth style, read, 'I'm like a great big barrel that feels like bursting if it doesn't have a vent. So I'm coming.' A spiritual revolution followed and the number of workmen who became Christians during these meetings changed the face of the factory.

Polly Wigglesworth, having witnessed the miraculous change in her husband's ministry, was soon convinced of the validity of his spiritual experience. She sought and received the fullness of the Spirit herself. That was the beginning of a short but effective partnership in a preaching ministry during which they shared pulpits.

On one occasion they went to a Methodist chapel in Shropshire. As Polly preached, the 'fire fell' and people were baptised in the Spirit in several places in the chapel simultaneously. It was a small country village and everyone around seemed to be greatly moved. But the next morning they encountered criticism. Nothing daunted, Wigglesworth walked around the village and went into the village store. Immediately a deep conviction of the Holy Spirit fell on the three people who were in the shop, and before he left they had committed their lives to Christ. He continued his walk and came across two women in a field carrying buckets. You can imagine their alarm when he shouted at them, 'Are you saved?' They dropped their buckets and fell on their knees seized by a strong conviction of sin. Smith knelt with them and prayed.

The significance of the story, of which similar details can be observed in many other instances, such as the time he was in a railway carriage en route for Cardiff and all the passengers in his compartment committed their lives to Christ, is this: Wigglesworth believed that when a man is filled with the presence of God he does not have to speak to bring conviction of sin. 'Wherever I went', he said, 'conviction seemed to be upon people.'

One day he was passing a large hotel in a town when two workmen in a 'horse and trap' (a two-wheeled passenger cart), went by. 'I have never seen men with such evil faces,' recalled Smith. 'They looked the very picture of the devil. I did not know who they were, but as they came near they cursed me and tried to slash me with their whips. It seemed like a whiff from the pit.' The men became so abusive and foul-mouthed that the scene attracted the attention of the proprietor of the hotel. He and some other people attacked Wigglesworth 'like mad dogs, cursing and swearing, though I had not spoken a word to them'. He stood his ground and thundered at them: 'In the name of Jesus, and in the power of the blood of Jesus, I drive you back into your den.' They immediately turned on their heels and rushed back into the hotel. But Wigglesworth had not finished with them. He followed them in and preached Christ to them.

Smith 'raises' his Lazarus

It was around this time that another inexplicable event took place in Wigglesworth's pilgrimage.

'One day in the early 1900s I went to the top of a high mountain in Wales for a time of prayer,' is how Wigglesworth began the story of this strange set of circumstances. 'The Lord's presence seemed to envelop and saturate me, reminding me of the transfiguration scene. I was impressed with the thought that the Lord's only purpose in giving us such glorious experiences is to prepare us for greater usefulness in the valley.'

Two years before this time two young Welshmen arrived at his house in Bradford and told him, 'We would not be surprised if the Lord brings you to Wales to raise our Lazarus.'

Now on the mountain top, Smith heard his Lord say to him. 'I want you to go and raise Lazarus.' He climbed down the mountain and sent a message to the Welsh valley that he was coming for Lazarus. When he arrived in the village, which was near Llanelli, South Wales, he was told, 'The moment you see him, you will be ready to go home. Nothing will hold you.' There was good cause for this negativism. Lazarus was 'nothing but a mass of bones with skin stretched over them. There was no life to be seen. Everything in him spoke of decay.'

Wigglesworth always said that the first task in his healing ministry, whether it be to one or a thousand, was to increase the people's faith in God. And this is what he set out to do for Lazarus. But Lazarus was different. He was a seasoned Christian. He knew it all. He had even taught it. He was the lay-pastor of the local assembly, an earnest, devout man, who had worked himself to the point of death in the mines, and at the same time had shepherded his flock in the village. But he no longer believed, nor did his people.

Smith invited the Welsh villagers to pray. They refused. They had lost all hope. They had prayed, but God had not healed. Lazarus was to die.

Two of the villagers had given a bed to Wigglesworth and his companion, so they both retired for the night. 'When I got

to bed it seemed as if the devil tried to place on me everything
that he had placed on that poor man. When I awoke I had a
cough and all the weakness of a tubercular patient. I rolled
out of bed ... and cried out to God to deliver me from the
power of the devil. I shouted loud enough to wake everybody
in the house, but nobody was disturbed. God gave victory,
and I got back in bed as free as ever. At five o'clock the Lord
awakened me and said, "Don't break bread until you break it
round my table." At six o'clock he gave me these words, "And
I will raise him up." I put my elbow into the fellow who was
sleeping with me and said, "Do you hear? The Lord says that
he will raise him up."'

Accompanied by seven others, Smith went to Lazarus.
They stood around his bed and made a chain by linking
hands. Lazarus was part of the chain too as Wigglesworth
and another brother each held one of his hands.

This, in Wigglesworth's words, is what happened.

'"We are just going to use the name of Jesus," I told them.
We knelt down and whispered that one word, "Jesus! Jesus!
Jesus!"

'The power of God fell and then it lifted. Five times the
power of God fell and then it remained. But the man in the
bed was unmoved. Two years previously, someone had come
along and had tried to raise him up, and the devil had used his
lack of success as a means of discouraging Lazarus.

'I said, "I don't care what the devil says. If God says he will
raise you up, it must be so. Forget everything else except what
God says about Jesus."

'The sixth time the power fell and the sick man's lips began
moving and the tears began to fall. I said, "The power of God
is here. It is yours to accept." Then he made a confession. "I
have been bitter in my heart, and I know I have grieved the
Spirit of God."'

Smith told Lazarus that he must repent and he would be
healed. He did, and he was.

'I have asked the Lord to never let me tell this story except
as it was, for I realise that God cannot bless exaggerations.

'As we again said, "Jesus! Jesus! Jesus!" the bed shook, and the man shook. I told the people who were with me that they could go downstairs. "This is all God. I'm not going to help him." I sat and watched that man get up and dress himself, and then we sang the doxology as he walked down the steps.'

Smith's simple, trusting faith in God

Bowland Street Mission became the 'turning around ground' for thousands of Bradford residents and the surrounding districts. It was inevitable that a prominent feature of its ministry to the inhabitants would include physical healing. To make this plain for all to see Wigglesworth erected a huge flagpole outside the Mission. On it he placed a flag with a red background on one side, and blue on the other. In large white letters on these backgrounds were the words, 'Christ died for our sins' and 'I am the Lord that healeth thee.'

Wigglesworth's faith was direct and simple. He had a childlike trust in his Lord. He took to heart the word of God and acted on it literally, sometimes to the discomfort of his fellow ministers. In these early days of his increasing faith he recognised that the word of God was written to show us how to act on the principles of faith. He was utterly devoted to the scriptures. Wherever he was, irrespective of the company, he would read his Bible. Always before eating, and always after a meal – and sometimes interrupting a meal.

This was highlighted when he visited Jerusalem and stayed at a missionary home which was under the direction of a Miss Radford. She had earned a worldwide reputation for order and efficiency and was a strict disciplinarian. Meals always started on time and ended on time, and no one, just no one, dared be late or change the programme. Nobody had the courage to contradict her and she knew it. But she hadn't previously encountered a character like Wigglesworth. On the occasion of Smith's visit, as was her custom, she stood up and announced the meal was to commence. Wigglesworth then stood up. In his normally stern voice he interrupted the lady, 'You've got to stop this lass. We have to listen to what Father has to say first.' Whereupon he took his little New Testament from his pocket and proceeded to read from it. Spiritual food to him, always took precedence over the natural. It was said that even the formidable Miss Radford was not the same after his visit.

He would frequently interlace his sermons with quotes, like: 'God's Word is – 1 supernatural in origin; 2 eternal in duration; 3 inexpressible in valour; 4 infinite in scope; 5 regenerative in power; 6 infallible in authority; 7 universal in application; 8 inspired in totality.' Then he would summarise: 'Read it through; write it down; pray it in; work it out; pass it on,' and conclude, 'The Word of God changes a man until he becomes an Epistle of God.'

The banquet

It was while reading his Bible on one occasion that Smith was struck by the words of Jesus in Luke 14: 12–14 about the material needs of the poor:

'[Jesus] said also to the man who had invited him, "When you give a dinner or a banquet, do not invite your friends or your brothers or your kinsmen or rich neighbours, lest they also invite you in return, and you be repaid. But when you give a feast, invite the poor, the maimed, the lame, the blind, and you will be blessed, because they cannot repay you. You will be repaid at the resurrection of the just."'

He and his wife accepted the words of Jesus as a directive to them in Bradford. True to form, he acted immediately.

Smith and Polly there and then devised a plan to put this into effect in an orderly manner. Well aware that if done haphazardly it would end in confusion, they employed two people to tour the poorer parts of Bradford announcing this event through loud-hailer and printed invitations. They invited the poor and sick to a large banquet, complete with

entertainment, in the Bowland Street Mission hall. The sight
was beyond description. People from all parts came, some in
wheelchairs, others on crutches, and the blind led by their
friends. First like ripples in tributaries, then a bubbling river.
'This was the best day of my life,' recounted Smith some time
later. 'I wept and wept and wept again. I wept because of the
great need. I wept for joy at the opportunity.'

The first thing Smith and Polly arranged was a 'first class
meal for everyone'. Everything provided was of the best.
'After they were filled, we gave them good entertainment, not
in the worldly sense, but the whole programme was surely
entertaining.'

The first person to take part in the programme was a man
who had been confined to a wheelchair for a very long time.
He had been healed by the power of God. He told his story.

Then came a woman who had been healed from an issue of
blood. She described how she was anointed with oil and that
Wigglesworth had then laid his hands on her as he prayed for
her healing. She told how she was due to be placed on an
operating table in the Bradford Hospital the next day. But
that was one engagement she was not going to keep, for God
had healed her.

The next person to come to the platform was a well-dressed
man. He walked up smartly and uprightly. It was hard to
imagine him as a paralysed person unable to do anything for
himself. The doctors had tried hard to cure the man, but had
failed. Quietly, but with restrained emotion, he described
what happened to him when prayed for by Smith
Wigglesworth.

It was right here that the audacious faith of Wigglesworth
began to reveal itself. After one and a half hours of
testimonies he addressed this varied assortment of the sick
and poor of Bradford: 'We have been entertaining you today,'
he began. 'But we are going to have another meeting next
Saturday, and you who today are bound, some of you in
wheelchairs, are going to entertain us by the stories of
freedom that you have received today by the name of Jesus

Christ.' Then he called out, 'Who wants to be healed?'

(Many Christians, as well as unbelievers, were critical of this approach. They described it as a cruel preying on the emotions of cripples and incurables. But to Smith it was a question of faith. His style of prayer for the sick and the evangelism of the unbeliever did not fit into a conventional mould. And he never changed.)

In response to his question, everyone present asked for healing. Who wouldn't? But though many were healed, others were not. That immediately poses the question, 'Why not?' It is a question I have heard debated in theological circles in many countries and for many years. We will look at it from Wigglesworth's viewpoint later.

Present at the banquet was a crippled lady whom Wigglesworth had collected personally. On his arrival at her home he found that the wheel of her 'bath chair' was broken and the rest of it was also in a bad state of repair. So, taking off his jacket, he started work on the chair and succeeded in making it mobile. They commenced their journey to Bowland Street but it broke down again. Such was Smith's faith, and the measure of his persistence, that he effected a temporary repair of the chair saying to the woman, 'Well, you'll never want it again anyhow.'

During the prayer that followed the banquet, he anointed the woman with oil – he had learnt to use just a drop and not the whole bottle by this time! Immediately he finished praying, the woman leapt to her feet. She excitedly jumped about the hall, completely healed. As Wigglesworth had foretold, she had no further use for the broken 'bath chair', but walked back home with Smith beside her laughing and praising God. 'I am a witness to the fact that she went up all the steps into her house, and into her bedroom, praising the Lord as she went,' he later reported to his congregation.

Another person healed was a young man who had suffered from epilepsy for eighteen years to such an extent that he could do no work. He had to depend on the meagre earnings of his father. His mother brought him to the banquet. He was instantly healed. Within two weeks he was bringing home wages from a nearby factory where he found employment.

Around this time Wigglesworth began to recognise more readily the different causes of physical sickness. For example, another young man present on this occasion was bent double like the woman in Luke 13. Recalling the incident, Luke 13:11 tells us that Jesus described the woman's illness as 'the spirit of infirmity'. Wigglesworth believed that to be an evil spirit. Instead of praying for the man, he rebuked the evil spirit and, using the name of Jesus, he commanded the spirit to leave the young man. Addressing himself to the crowd of sick people, he said, 'Christ in his healing ministry said he was working the works of God and that if we believe, we could also do the works of God. Christ cast out the spirit of infirmity. So I cast out the spirit of infirmity in the name of Jesus Christ.' And immediately, the young man's body was straightened and he stood erect in front of the people. When he later told the Assemblies of God Church in Royston, Yorkshire, of this healing he added, 'Never cast out an evil spirit twice. If you do the devil will laugh at you. He will know that you have no power.'

One other healing demands a place here. A father had carried to the meeting his crippled son who had been encased in thin iron from his head to his feet to hold his little body in one position. The Mission hall was filled to capacity, so there was no room to move with ease. However, the father of the boy was determined to get his son to Smith Wigglesworth. In desperation the man lifted his boy above the heads of the people and he was passed from one row of people to another until he was placed at Wigglesworth's feet. Again Smith turned to his little bottle of olive oil and, following a short prayer, anointed the young lad. Immediately the boy's body shuddered under the impact of divine power, and he cried out, 'Daddy, daddy. It's going all over me. It's going all over me!' Feverish hands unclipped the metal cage and released the lad. He stood before the people completely healed.

Smith's 'ministry of faith'

Wigglesworth was now developing a ministry of faith that later earned him the title from his friends, 'Apostle of Faith'. He would make outstanding claims, and those hearing them for the first time would wonder how he found the audacity to make them.

Smith believed in different kinds of gifts of faith. For example, he cited Rees Howells, founder of the Bible College of Wales, as a man of faith for finance, whereas Smith did not claim to have such a gift. His gift was for healing. But he also recognised that you had to cultivate faith in God. This is not to be confused with positive thinking or auto-suggestion.

In answer to questions about faith he would direct the enquirer to the word of God. He would point out that in the act of receiving the word faith springs up in our hearts. It is a faith that begins with believing in Christ's sacrifice on Calvary, and it involves believing that he not only took upon himself our sins but our sicknesses. He is our life today. Then Smith would quote the verse, 'First the blade, then the ear, then the full corn'. He would say that faith must grow out of clean and pure soil, moistened by the Spirit of God, and exercised by the individual. 'Faith is an act', is a phrase he carried around the world.

Fear looks, faith jumps

'I must have a ministry of faith,' he said. 'I must have a clothing for this ministry of faith ... Let me speak of three classes of faith. Good ... Better ... Best. God has the best. In Pentecost I find some people are satisfied with "tongues". That would never satisfy me. I want the Person who gives them. I am the hungriest man that you ever saw. I want all that God has. Without God giving me I am a perfectly spoiled baby. "Father," I say. "You will have to give me."' Then with a twinkle in his eye, adding, 'Be careful of your friends and relations, they are always a damp rag or a wet blanket. God wants us to lean on him, and go on with him and dare to believe him.' And, 'If the thoughts and intentions of our hearts are not loyal to God, or if we desire something else more than the will of God, faith will be hindered . . . If I wait for power I have mistaken the position. If I could only feel the power? We have been too much on that line. God is waiting for you to act – Jesus was perfect activity – He lived in the realm of divine appointment.'

One other comment of his on the same subject I found helpful. Preaching on Mark 4:40, 'And Jesus said unto them, Why were you so fearful? How is it that you have no faith?', he said, 'Nothing is plainer there than that the Lord Jesus looked upon their spirit of fearfulness as evidence of their lack of faith. There cannot be rest where there is fearfulness.'

It has to be acknowledged that his exegesis was often questioned by his contemporaries, and especially when he told the students at the Men's Training Home, King Edward Road, Hackney, London (one of the first Pentecostal schools in the United Kingdom), 'If you ask God seven times for the same thing, six times are in unbelief.' And, 'If the Spirit does not move me, I move the Spirit.' Commenting on this short period when Wigglesworth was in charge of the school, Donald Gee wrote that it was an experience 'that students at that time will never forget'.

Questionable though some of his statements may have been, few will disagree with this: 'Great faith is a product of great fights. Great testimonies are the outcome of great tests. Great triumphs can only come after great trials.'

12 'Till death us do part'?

Raising the dead

William Hibbert in his book *Smith Wigglesworth – The Secret of his Power* states, 'I know of fourteen occasions when the dead were raised during Wigglesworth's ministry.' He then cites two instances. Many leaders of Wigglesworth's day questioned the veracity of these reports. Are we right to report what we have not witnessed?

Have you heard of the publisher's dilemma? I was confronted with one when I was Managing Director of Coverdale House Publishers. One day a manuscript arrived on my desk containing accounts related by Mel Tari of miraculous events that had taken place in Indonesia. It was called, *Like a Mighty Wind*. I read it and reread it several times. I could not bring myself to reject it. On the other hand I could not persuade myself to accept it. This was unusual for me – I was never slow in making decisions.

One day I had a visit from Dr Kenneth Taylor (the translator of the Living Bible), who also happened to be my 'boss'. He saw the book on my desk and asked if I was going to publish it. I explained my dilemma. He suggested I went to Indonesia to check the reports. 'What, with all those islands?' I protested. Then he asked how I would have dealt with the Acts of the Apostles if Luke had sent his manuscript to me. I published Mel Tari's book.

What should be the publisher's or writer's criteria in these circumstances? They certainly have a duty to be accurate and honest. I also believe that they should avoid sensationalism if it is only for the sake of being sensational. My first response is to ascertain the integrity of the author. When I am satisfied of that, I am ready to align myself with him.

When the evangelists write that Jesus brought Lazarus back from the dead, I believe them to be true. When Luke writes that Peter and John told a lame man to walk, and that the man did just that, I believe Luke to be true. When I read that Jesus walked on water or that he made the best kind of wine from the most ordinary kind of water in a split second of time, then I believe the account to be true. Why? Because I believe the author. I have faith in him. The credibility is right there.

Were the dead brought back to life through Wigglesworth's ministry? I went to the United States, to Springfield, Missouri, and was given access to the excellent archives of the Assemblies of God. My first day made my trip worthwhile. I discovered a verbatim account from Wigglesworth himself which was recorded during his visit to Belfast, Northern Ireland, in 1926.

'One day at 11 o'clock I saw a woman with a tumour. She could live out one day. I said, "Do you want to live?" She could not speak. She just moved her finger. I said, "In the Name of Jesus." And I poured on the oil. (Mr Fisher was with me.) He said, "She's gone." O the place of rest by faith. The place beyond all. Without faith one dare not think of the righteousness which is of God. Stand with God. The righteousness of faith has resurrection in it, and moves on resurrection lines.

'A little blind girl led me to the bedside. Compassion broke me up for the child's sake. I had said, "Lift your finger." Carrying the mother across the room I put her up against the wardrobe. I held her there. I said, "In the Name of Jesus, death come out." Like a fallen tree, leaf after leaf, her body began moving – upright instead of lifeless. Her feet touched the floor. "In Jesus' Name walk!" I said. She did, back to bed.

'I told this story in the Assembly. There was a doctor there. He was sceptical. He saw her. She said it is all true. "I was in heaven. I saw countless numbers all like Jesus. He pointed and I knew I had to go. Then I heard a voice saying, 'Walk in the Name of Jesus.'"'

'The power of his resurrection. The righteousness which is of God by faith.'

The intriguing thing about that story is that we do not hear of healing for the little blind girl!

What happens when the one you love dies?

The year was 1913. Smith and Polly were in their early fifties. Life was good. The business was very successful. The Mission was thriving with spiritual activity. Smith was now travelling to other cities and on this particular evening he had to leave for Glasgow, Scotland, for a preaching appointment, but he did not go. An event took place that was to change the whole course of his life. He 'lost' the 'best girl in the world', as he called her.

While preaching on the 'beatitudes' some years later, Wigglesworth gave this personal account of what happened.

'"Blessed are the poor in spirit: for theirs is the kingdom of heaven." This is one of the richest places into which Jesus brings us. The poor have a right to everything in heaven. "Theirs is." Dare you believe it? Yes. I dare. I believe, I know, that I was very poor. When God's Spirit comes in as the ruling, controlling power of the life, he gives us God's revelation of our inward poverty, and shows us that God has come with one purpose, to bring heaven's best to earth, and that with Jesus he will indeed "freely give us all things".

'An old man and an old woman had lived together for seventy years. Someone said to them, "You must have seen many clouds during those days." They replied, "Where do the showers come from? You never get showers without clouds." It is only the Holy Spirit who can bring us to the place of realisation of our poverty; but, every time he does it, he opens the windows of heaven and the showers of blessing fall.

'But I must recognise the difference between my own spirit and the Holy Spirit. My own spirit can do certain things on natural lines, can even weep and pray and worship, but it is all on a human plane. And we must not depend on our own human thoughts and activities or on our own personality. If the baptism [in the Holy Spirit] means anything to you, it should bring you to the death of the ordinary, where you are no longer putting faith in your own understanding; but, conscious of your own poverty, you are ever yielded to the Spirit. Then it is, that your body becomes filled with heaven on earth.

'"Blessed are they that mourn: for they shall be comforted." People get a wrong idea of mourning. Over in Switzerland they have a day set apart to take wreaths to graves. I laughed at the people's ignorance and said, "Why are you spending time around the graves? The people you love are not there. All that taking of flowers to the graves is not faith at all." Those who died in Christ are gone to be with him, which, Paul said, "is far better".

'My wife once said to me, "Smith, you watch me when I'm preaching. I get so near to heaven when I'm preaching that some day I'll be off."

'One night she was preaching and when she had finished, off she went. I was going to Glasgow and had said goodbye to her before she went to the meeting. As I was leaving the house, the doctor and policeman met me at the door and told me that she had fallen dead at the Mission door. I knew she had got what she wanted. I could not weep, but I was in tongues, praising the Lord. On natural lines she was everything to me; but I could not mourn on natural lines, but just laughed in the Spirit.

'The house was soon filled with people. The doctor said, "She is dead, and we can do no more for her." I went up to her lifeless corpse and commanded death to give her up, and she came back to me for a moment. Then God said to me, "She is mine; her work is done." I knew what he meant.

'They laid her in the coffin. And I brought my sons and my daughter into the room and said, "Is she there?" They said, "No, father." I said, "We will cover her up."

'If you go mourning the loss of loved ones who have gone to be with Christ, I say it in love to you, you have never had the revelation of what Paul spoke of when he shows us that it is better to go than to stay. We read this in Scripture. But the trouble is that people will not believe it. When you believe God, you will say, "Whatever it is, it is all right. If you want to take the one I love, it is all right Lord." Faith removes all tears of self-pity.'

Throughout this experience Smith's faith remained unshaken, and some of his associates reckoned that a new depth in his ministry became evident.

Two years later he was to receive yet another severe blow. His youngest son, George, was to die. This greatly puzzled him.

Two anomalies

There was also the anomalous case of his only daughter, Alice. She was stone deaf, and remained that way throughout her life.

Ruth Steelberg Carter tells of the time when Wigglesworth was holding a meeting in Sacramento. As he preached healing and faith Alice was, as usual, seated near him. 'His glasses got all tangled up at the end of a chain. So he called, "Halice." But Alice couldn't hear him. So he shouted this time, "Halice, come and help me." She still didn't hear him. So he shouted louder. "Halice, Halice." And the people in the congregation couldn't help but find this amusing. Here was this man, a great man of faith, but his daughter was deaf and he had to have glasses.' When asked about his daughter's deafness, he would mischievously reply, 'It's her lack of faith.' But did he really mean it? There is no record of him attempting a further explanation.

Wigglesworth was devoted to his daughter. She and her husband James Salter were his constant companions on his preaching tours following their missionary service in Africa. Her presence appeared to be a contradiction of his healing ministry. Was it his equivalent of Paul's thorn in the flesh?

Was it to keep him humble and to remind him that the prerogative for healing is with God, not man? His daughter-in-law Florence, wife of Seth, knew him better than most. As a little girl in Bradford, she had become a Christian through his ministry. As we sat together in her home in Southport, Lancashire, reminiscing about Wigglesworth, she expressed the opinion that 'Alice's deafness seemed to teach him patience. He was marvellous with her. He would have her read the Bible and open his correspondence. This made him patient with others. He grew more tolerant. Because he did have dreadful tempers, especially if the meals were not to his liking. But all this changed after his baptism.'

With Alice he was always full of compassion. As was his custom, he would take his New Testament from his pocket and read from it, but the only way she could know what he was saying was to lip read. With great concern he would turn his face towards her so that she could understand what he was saying, and feel part of what he was doing. His grandson Leslie Wigglesworth said to me, 'You could almost feel the agony. It was something he had to bear. Yet it didn't make any difference to his faith in his Master.' It was at times like this that he would suddenly stretch out his hands towards his daughter and pray for her healing, a healing which she was never to experience.

The other paradox in Wigglesworth's life was his poor eyesight. Once when challenged about this by a critic he impishly replied, 'Go and ask Elisha why he had a bald head.' But in private he had another explanation.

The late Wesley Steelberg, Ruth's first husband and General Superintendent of the American Assemblies of God, noticing that on occasions Wigglesworth would wear glasses to read his New Testament decided to ask him for an explanation. 'Brother Wigglesworth,' he began somewhat timorously, 'you have such great faith, but I want you to forgive me for this: I said in my heart, "If he has such great faith, why is he wearing glasses?"' Wigglesworth began to weep. Then he said, 'Son, I'm so glad you told me what you were thinking. That's why I'm wearing glasses today. Years ago I saw a man who believed that God could heal and he was wearing glasses. And I criticised him in my heart. But I didn't confess it like you have. I'm so glad you came to me, because I didn't do as you have. And all of my life since then I've had to wear glasses.'

The Christian's attitude to trials

As we bring down the shutters on this sad part of Smith Wigglesworth's life it would be fitting to quote his attitude to trials, the ultimate of which is death.

'Whatever befalls you as you abide in Christ see that the good hand of God is upon you, so that you won't lose your inheritance. Every trial is a gift – every burden a place of strength.'

'If you comprehend the truth of this word, "It is far better for me to go," which Paul realised was true, you will never take a pill nor use a plaster. You would never do anything to save yourself from going if you believed it was better to go.'

13 Ever-increasing circles

Wigglesworth hits the headlines

I have just acquired an unusual print. It is a copy of the front
page of England's most widely read national daily newspaper, the *Daily Mirror*. It is unusual not only because it is
dated Friday, May 16th 1913, but because of its front page
story. Front page space in the British press is not the usual
place for religious news, even when it's Billy Graham. But
Smith Wigglesworth could never be described as 'usual'.

Under the headlines: 'Five Pentecostalists baptised in the
sea: woman falls prostrate after immersion in icy water,' are
four large pictures of baptismal scenes in the North Sea which
show Wigglesworth in 'Extraordinary scenes... at Roker,
near Sunderland, when three women and two men – the latest
converts of the Pentecostalists, who are holding their annual
convention – were baptised in the sea yesterday. The
ceremony took place in the early morning, and so cold was
the water that the women almost collapsed from shock.
While the converts were in the sea those on the beach danced
wildly about, waving their arms and singing hymns.'

The caption to the fourth photograph reads: 'Mr
Wigglesworth of Bradford, who performed the ceremony,
offering up a prayer on the beach before entering the water
with the converts.'

Wigglesworth had also made news the previous year when
reporters from the *Sunderland Daily Echo* were present at
two of his meetings at the Rev Alexander Boddy's church, All
Saints', Monkwearmouth, Sunderland. On Friday, May 31st
1912, a lengthy report detailed several healings including the
deliverance of two people who had been demon-possessed.

The report tells of how Smith Wigglesworth confronted a man who had been demented for a long time and was 'unmanageable'.

Wigglesworth had been to an early morning prayer meeting and was taking a stroll along the seafront when he saw 'the man with only his trousers on' rushing towards the sea. 'I met him' Wigglesworth was reported as saying, 'and in the name of Jesus I commanded the demon to come out of the man. He fell full length in the middle of the road and God delivered him instantly. He rose up with tears in his eyes, and said "I'm a new man. I'm free."'

The 'call' to North America

1914 was a memorable year for most people. It certainly was for Smith Wigglesworth, but in a way different from most, for it was the beginning of his international ministry.

Smith was restless. Polly was no longer with him and his business was no longer the attraction it had been. For no obvious reason he was beginning to be drawn to North America: 'The Lord moved upon me in England to tell the people that I was going to America through Canada.'

Wigglesworth, believing this to be the prompting of the Holy Spirit, talked to his master in the only way he knew how. 'Well, Lord. You know you will have to do a miracle and you must do it sharp if you mean business, because I want to be in haste about this if it is your plan. The first thing is, you know I have a bad memory. You will have to work a miracle there. The next thing is, you will have to find me all the money because I cannot leave my children without money. And I have no money to go, so you will have to find a lot.'

Money started to come in a large and fast fashion. 'It was amazing how the Lord began to drop it.' It was coming so fast that he told the people that so much money was coming he was sure he was going. And then the money stopped coming.

'There was no more dropping,' was his description.

Quickly recognising that he had grieved the Holy Spirit he repented, saying, 'If you begin again to show me it is your will, I won't tell anybody.' Then the gifts commenced again, 'falling as gently as rain'.

By now his children were getting disturbed. One of them remonstrated, 'Father, mother has gone to heaven. It will be very lonely without you.' At that moment the door bell rang. 'George, go answer the front door,' said Wigglesworth. Adding, 'And let the Lord speak to you through this ring at the door whether I have to go or not.'

There was a letter.

'Now George,' said his father, 'open the letter and whatever there is in the letter, read it and let that suffice you whether I have to go or not.' George opened the letter. The letter had come a long distance and had been posted six weeks earlier, as Smith said, 'just about the time I repented'. It contained a cheque for £25.

'What about it, George?' asked Wigglesworth. 'Father, I won't say anything else,' replied the boy. And money continued to come from the most unexpected quarters adding to Wigglesworth's conviction that God required him in North America.

Europe was in a state of unrest. France had ambitions on Alsace-Lorraine, which they wanted to get back from the Germans. The Germans had their eyes on the Mediterranean and economic control of the Near East. The Russians were seeking to dominate the Balkans as their outlet to the Mediterranean. Those with keen political eyesight saw the war clouds on the horizon.

Most Pentecostalists were pacifists. And this is where the disenchantment with the man used by God to bring Pentecost to England began. Alexander Boddy, as a loyal Anglican priest, was strongly in favour of active participation in the war when it came. On the other wing was A S Booth-Clibborn, who came from a Quaker family. He was equally strong in his opposition. As the soldiers marched to the front

line singing, 'It's a long, long way to Tipperary,' he supplied
alternative words to that popular tune:

> It's a straight, straight, way that leads to glory
> It's the way of the Cross;
> But it shines evermore before me,
> While I'm 'counting all but dross'!
> Farewell, sin and sorrow,
> Goodbye anxious care;
> It's a long, long way that leads to glory,
> But my heart's right there!

As all this was taking place Wigglesworth was on the high
seas bound for Canada en route for the United States of
America.

Canadian incidents

Two Canadian events are worth mentioning, although it is
uncertain whether they occured on the first or second visit.

Following one of his meetings in Toronto a 'big, fine, tall
man' arrived at the home where Smith was staying. 'Three
years ago my nerves became shattered,' he told him. 'I can't
sleep. I have lost my business. I have lost everything. I am not
able to sleep at all and my life is one of misery.'

Wigglesworth placed his hands on the man's shoulders,
looked him straight in the eye (an unnerving experience for
anyone!) and told him: 'Go home, and sleep in the name of
Jesus.' The man hesitated. Smith repeated his command. He
turned around but seemed reluctant to go. 'Go!' bellowed
Wigglesworth into the man's ear, and thrust him out of the
door.

Early next day there was a telephone call. It was from the
man who could not sleep. He said, 'Tell Mr Wigglesworth I
slept all night. And I would like to come and see him at once.'
When he arrived he thanked Wigglesworth profusely saying,

'I'm a new man. I feel I have a new life. But now, can you get my money back?' Without a moment's hesitation Smith replied, 'Everything!' 'How?' asked the man. He refused to give him an immediate answer. Instead he said, 'Come to the meeting tonight and I'll tell you.'

That night Wigglesworth preached on the holiness of God and the abomination of sin. It was a remarkably powerful meeting, and the man came under great conviction. When the sermon was finished, the man rose from his seat and made for the altar. But he fell prostrate before he got there. Before he left the church that night, he made his peace with God. 'All his past failures had come through a lack of the knowledge of God,' was Wigglesworth's opinion. The man's life underwent a thorough transformation. His business improved. He later recovered all his losses, in fulfilment of Smith's promise to him.

As he travelled on by train, Wigglesworth found himself in a compartment where there were two sick people, a mother and her daughter. He had his briefcase on his knees. Suddenly he said to the two women, 'Look, I've something in this bag that will cure every case in the world. It has never been known to fail.' Their interest could not fail to be aroused. So he went on to tell them about this remedy he had discovered that had never failed to remove all disease and sickness. Finally, though somewhat timidly, they found the courage to ask for a dose.

With a reassuring smile on his face, Wigglesworth opened his bag and produced his famous little Bible, and read: 'I am the Lord that healeth thee.' He then developed his regular theme of faith in God. 'As I talked about this wonderful physician, the faith of both mother and daughter went out toward him,' said Smith. Before they left the train, he prayed with them, and they were completely healed.

On another occasion a woman said to him, 'I have not been able to smell for twenty years. Can you do anything for me?' 'You shall smell tonight,' Wigglesworth replied. After the evening meeting she ran all the way home, and although a mouth-watering meal was on the table, 'she would not touch a thing'. She said. 'I'm having a feast of smelling!'

Wigglesworth in the United States

Eventually Wigglesworth crossed over the border into the United States. He had no preaching appointments and was unknown. It was summer time and most of the Christian activities had been transferred to summer camps. He was close to one such camp, a place called Cazadero, in northern California.

On arrival he introduced himself to the conveners of the camp, Mr and Mrs Montgomery. They immediately took a liking to him, and invited him to be one of the speakers that night.

Several ministers had already been booked to speak. It was a long meeting; at the end the leader of the meeting turned to Wigglesworth without any welcome in his voice and said, somewhat curtly, 'Now it's your turn. Are you ready?' 'Always,' responded Wigglesworth.

He shed himself of his coat and advanced to the front of the platform. Such was the anointing of the Holy Spirit upon him, this uneducated and unpolished plumber from Yorkshire, that he held the congregation spellbound. The Montgomerys, their faith in their visitor confirmed, invited him to join the panel of camp speakers for the convention. He ministered there both morning and evening for the remaining three weeks.

'This man has a message of faith that is outstanding,' was the general comment of the campers, 'and we want to hear him.'

Wigglesworth's preaching style

Wigglesworth would frequently begin his messages with an

invitation, 'All who believe in prayer, put one hand up. All who believe in praying aloud, put two hands up. Now, everybody stand up and do it, and get what your heart desires.' When criticised about this he would reply, 'This is not a Wigglesworth invention. It is in the first book of the Bible. Abraham did it. It is in the last book of the Bible. An angel did it. What's more it's in the middle of the Bible. Moses, Aaron, David, Ezekiel – they all did it. It meant all the difference between winning or losing a battle.' Then he would quote Paul's injunction in 1 Timothy 2:8, 'I want men everywhere to lift up holy hands in prayer, without anger or disputing' (NIV).

When closing his meeting he would often introduce a series of challenges to his audience, with such questions as: 'Who wants to get nearer to God? Who would like a special blessing?' Then he would say, 'Let everyone who is hungry for God stand on his feet.' When they were standing he would give a general invitation for everyone to move forward just one pace. To all who responded he would say, 'Now, that shows you mean business.' After that he would ask everyone who had taken that one pace forward to join him at the front of the hall if they really wanted God's blessing.

With the seekers surrounding him he would invite them to answer some more questions: 'Who will lift up hands in faith and ask God for something?' 'Now, thank God for it.' 'Now again, ask God for something.' 'Now, thank God.'

He would send his hearers away with these terse statements: 'Ask for what you want. Believe, receive. And thank God for it.' However, he was not enthusiastic about long periods of prayer. Certainly he did not practise them. When asked if prayer could ever be ineffective or spoilt, he replied: 'Yes. If you begin in the Spirit, and when you have finished, you then go on in the flesh.'

At other times he would provoke people by dismissing long periods of intercession, saying, 'I never pray for more than half-an-hour'; but after a short pause he would add, 'I never go longer than half-an-hour without praying.'

In his own way he regularly departed from the cliché, frequently overstating his point. Was this deliberate? Who knows? But we do know he had a strong sense of humour. One day on a visit to the Chamber of Horrors at Madame Tussauds, where his name is recorded alongside the former public executioner Berry, he entered the exhibition area and stood alongside the model of Berry. Before he could move, a group of American tourists came into the Chamber. So he remained where he was, perfectly still. After reading the notices and looking at the models the group moved on with the exception of one of the female members of the party. As the woman looked at him Wigglesworth could not resist the temptation. He winked at her. She nearly fainted. And to make matters worse for her, the other members of the party refused to believe her story.

Maybe it was due to his desire to shake his listeners out of the commonplace that he once said, 'It is absolute infidelity and unbelief to pray about anything in the word of God. The word of God is not to be prayed about. The word of God has to be received.' And, 'Do more believing and less begging.'

14   Back Home

Conventions and revival meetings

After spending the winter months in North America, Wigglesworth returned to the United Kingdom in time for his Easter Convention in Bradford in 1915. His itinerant ministry continued, beginning with London's first Whitsuntide Convention of the Pentecostalists. It was arranged and chaired by Cecil Polehill of the 'Cambridge Seven'. Also on the platform that day were two well-known pioneering evangelists, George and Stephen Jeffreys. Donald Gee, reporting the event, wrote, 'The outstanding ministry of Mr Wigglesworth was the outstanding feature of the Convention. Many were baptised in the Spirit, and many were healed.'

One of the memorable annual events in his ministry in the United Kingdom was his role as chairman of the Preston Convention. Following the demise of the Sunderland conventions, similar events developed in Preston in the north at Easter and London in the south at Whitsuntide.

Another significant Christian of this period was Thomas Myerscough, a Preston estate agent and a very devout man. He was the leader of a small group of believers who met regularly to seek a deeper spiritual experience. They began to hear reports of great blessings being experienced by some Christians in nearby Lytham, so they decided to attend one of these 'revival meetings'.

'On leaving the meeting,' said Myerscough, 'we stood together in the road, each of us testifying we had never before heard such glorifying of the Lord Jesus, nor such fervency in prayer.' For the following nine months the Preston group studied the scriptures relating to gifts of the Holy Spirit and became convinced that they were for today. Myerscough was at the Sunderland Convention the following Whitsun and was baptised in the Holy Spirit. Through Myerscough there began a chain of events that was to shape the twentieth-century work of the Holy Spirit in and beyond the United Kingdom.

Arising from the work of Myerscough and his group were several works of God. First of all a Bible School was established, with Myerscough – an outstanding Bible expositor – as the principal. The future leaders of the British Pentecostal movements were trained there, including George Jeffreys and E J Phillips. Two other results of the Preston group were the Congo Evangelistic Mission – pioneered by two young men from Preston, W F B Burton and James Salter (who was later to become Wigglesworth's son-in-law and travelling companion) – and the renowned Preston Easter Convention.

Smith Wigglesworth in the chair

The largest buildings in Preston were hired for the Preston Easter Convention as each year thousands flocked to the meetings. Pentecostal leaders throughout the world came to speak and Wigglesworth sat in the chair. The only meeting in which he preached was the Sunday afternoon which was set aside as a divine healing meeting. To readers who have only known of him as a preacher, it may come as a surprise to learn that he could excel himself in grace and wisdom as a chairman, for it was no mean task to maintain order over an excited and vibrant crowd of enthusiastic Pentecostals, especially as they were quick to condemn anything done to limit their new-found freedom. These conventions had an 'indefinable difference' from other Christian events, said

Donald Gee. They had 'an individual liberty, a simple spirituality, a lack of ministerial formality, an emphasis upon the distinctive testimony of the Pentecostal Movement, a place of spiritual gifts, an utter abandon that can only be summed up as peculiarly and uncompromisingly "Pentecostal".'

Such Pentecostal meetings were not easy to control. But, if he felt it necessary, Smith was capable of reproving the great as well as the small. There was the time when a famous Welsh preacher in full rhetorical flight, flailing his arms like a windmill out of control, and with sweat pouring down his face, did not appear to know how to stop. Wigglesworth slowly rose from his seat at the back of the platform, from where it was his custom to convene these meetings, and sauntered over to the preacher at the rostrum. Putting his hand on his shoulder he was heard to say in a stage whisper, 'Sit down brother, you're killing yourself and us!'

15   Travelling in Europe

It was not long after the war ended that Smith Wigglesworth was invited to conduct meetings in Scandinavia, Switzerland and France. This invitation was to be the start of a worldwide ministry.

France

One of his first meetings in France was arranged by Madame Debat of Paris. It took place in a village near Chartres. French Protestants are notoriously cautious, being very reserved in theology, so four of their ministers were 'on hand to examine' this stranger's teaching.

Once again the unusual happened. The tranquillity of this French village was disturbed by the clatter of a team of oxen and the harsh noises of the wheels of the wagon they were pulling. On the wagon was a stretcher bearing a sick man. He was suffering from a cancerous growth in his stomach and he could not eat.

News had reached him of the remarkable answers to prayer that had accompanied Wigglesworth's ministry, and that this English evangelist was to pray for the sick in this village. So he came, 'full of faith'. As evidence, he had with him in the cart a basket of different kinds of food. When asked if the food was for his journey to the meetings, he replied, 'No, because I cannot eat now. But I'm going to be healed, so I shall consume these provisions on the return journey!' He was instantly healed. The four 'examining' theologians needed no further evidence; convinced that this was the work of God, one of them exclaimed, 'I am under an open heaven.'

Parts of France had heard the Pentecostal message as early as 1909, but largely due to the war and the dispersal of huge sections of the population this had not been received as widely as in the United Kingdom. Prevented from full development during these war years, the young French Pentecostal assemblies were now only too pleased and ready to welcome Wigglesworth. His travels ultimately took him to Le Havre. Here at the Ruban Bleu, a temperance hotel owned by Madame Hélène Biolley, a centre for Pentecostal meetings was established following his visit. This became a starting place for many of the Pentecostal leaders in France.

Switzerland

The picturesque city of Lausanne, situated close to Lake Geneva, although it is in the French-speaking part of Switzerland is also a railway crossing-point for the Swiss from the German and Italian parts. It is also a significant resting place on the international highway across the Simplon Pass to Milan.

It was to Lausanne, in response to an invitation from a group of Swiss Christians, that Wigglesworth made his way from France. They had heard of blessings through his ministry and, being hungry for God to do the same for them, had arranged a series of meetings. Madame Debat of Paris travelled with Smith as his interpreter. Following these meetings she was to report outstanding scenes of spiritual awakening and many astonishing healings. In addition to those in Lausanne, he conducted meetings in Geneva, Vevey, Morges and Neuchâtel. He also held meetings in German-speaking cities including Zurich, Berne and Basle.

In her account of the healings, Madame Debat tells of the complete healing of a man in Lausanne who had been born blind and whose wife was in an advanced stage of tuberculosis (considered uncurable in those days). Also at

Lausanne there was a child who had a new eye given to him. At Morges a healing took place similar to the one recorded in Acts 4. A crippled man leapt from his wheelchair and jumped about the hall. He then walked home along the cobbled streets of this quaint lakeside town followed by a crowd of boys, one pushing his chair.

In one place a woman with an ugly cancerous growth on her face came to the front of the hall for prayer. Wigglesworth turned her towards the congregation and said, 'Look at her. She will be here tomorrow night and you will see what God has done for her.' Then he laid hands on her, anointed her with oil, and commanded the sickness to leave her. He always held a firm conviction that cancer was a special work of the devil. Nothing appeared to happen, but the next night she was back, and stood in front of the people without a scar or mark on her face. She was completely healed.

Smith Wigglesworth was always fair game for the sceptics, who would have other explanations for these healings. In Neuchâtel a Dr Emil Lanz, a well-known Berne dentist, thinking they were artificial, challenged Wigglesworth to show him his teeth. He discovered that not only were they natural, they were in sound condition. As a result of this incident Dr Lanz became committed to the Pentecostal testimony. On a visit to London, when speaking of these meetings, he said, 'We have seen great things in Switzerland in the last three years, and many new gatherings have been raised up in both French-speaking and German-speaking Switzerland through the ministry of Smith Wigglesworth. Many, many of our people have received the great Pentecostal blessing of the baptism of the blessed Holy Spirit with signs following, and we are deeply grateful for this. Two years ago in Berne, we had only fifteen coming to the meetings. Today we have a great gathering and a beautiful hall. Every Sunday night many are being saved, healed and baptised in the Holy Spirit.'

However, there was strong opposition by the authorities in several places. Wigglesworth was imprisoned twice during these visits. In the first town where he had been arrested, because of complaints by doctors about his healing meetings, a woman well known to the police for her drunkenness had been healed. The minister of the church presented the woman to the police and said, 'This woman came to one of our meetings in a state of drunkenness. While she was there in this condition Mr Wigglesworth laid his hands on her and asked God to deliver her. Her body was broken out in terrible sores. But God healed her. And she was also delivered from her drunkenness.' Then the woman spoke. 'God saved my soul,' she told the officers. 'I am no longer a slave to drink.' Impressed by the obvious change in this notorious character, the senior officer said, 'I refuse to stop this kind of work. Somebody else will have to arrest this man.'

On the second occasion a police officer came to his cell in the middle of the night and, without any explanation, told him to collect his belongings and leave. Imagine the officer's surprise when Wigglesworth refused. 'No,' he said. 'I'll only go on one condition. That every officer in this place gets down on his knees and I'll pray for you.'

Sweden

A few months before the outpouring of the Holy Spirit in Sunderland in September 1907, a Baptist pastor in Sweden, Lewi Pethrus, had casually picked up his Stockholm newspaper and read of a remarkable revival that had broken out in Norway. The Swedish minister felt a tug in his heart as he read the report.

The next day he was on his way to Oslo determined not to return until he too had received the baptism in the Holy Spirit. He was not to be disappointed. He met Thomas Barratt and the two men united in prayer. Pethrus received the promise of Acts 1:8, and that was the beginning of a unique work of the Spirit in Sweden which has been unequalled in the rest of the world. However, the Swedish authorities were not so disposed to welcome the healing ministry of Smith Wigglesworth when he arrived in 1920.

Stockholm was, and is, famed for the beauty and physical characteristics of its situation. The coast is thickly fringed with islands which provide many recreational activities for those privileged to live there. Small wonder that the residents have an inbred confidence and independence from the rest of Europe. The city was originally founded as a fortress, and in later years commanded all the foreign commerce of that part of Sweden. Into this well-endowed and self-sufficient city came this uneducated and uncultured Yorkshire workman, so it was not surprising that many looked upon Wigglesworth's mission as an effrontery to their elegance. But such was the divine commission given to him, and recognised by him, that soon his exploits were to become news to no less a person than the King of Sweden.

Wigglesworth was accompanied on some of his visits by Madame Lewini, formerly a well-known actress in Scandinavia, who wrote to her friends in Copenhagen: 'It was wonderful to notice, as the ministry continued, the effect upon the people as the power of the Lord came over them. Some lifted their hands crying, "I am healed! I am healed!" Some fell on the platform overpowered by the power of the Holy Spirit and had to be helped down. A young blind girl, as she was ministered to, cried out, "Oh, how many windows there are in this hall."'

In spite of the size of the buildings where the meetings were held, it was impossible to accommodate all the people, frequently necessitating police control. Crowds of people waited for many hours to gain entrance to the meetings, and any places becoming vacant by those who left early were immediately taken by those who had had to wait outside.

At the end of one of the meetings a man supported by two crutches, his whole body shaking with palsy, was lifted to the platform. Wigglesworth prayed for him. Though he continued to shake, he was able to walk with the help of only one crutch. Encouraged by Wigglesworth, in his special manner, the man discarded the remaining crutch as he continued to walk around the platform. Then he walked around the auditorium until his body stopped shaking. His healing electrified the atmosphere. A woman screamed. Smith told her to be quiet. Instead she jumped on a chair, and cried out almost hysterically, 'I'm healed! I'm healed! I had a cancer in my mouth. And I was unsaved. But during this meeting as I listened to the word of God, the Lord has saved me and healed me of this cancer!' And she continued to shout, 'I am saved! I am healed!' And the people cried and laughed together with her.

In the same meeting, another woman who was unable to walk, and who sat in a wheelchair, received the laying-on-of-hands. Smith prayed with his customary faith and authority. Dazed, the woman stood to her feet. Looking around at the people, she thought she was in a dream. Suddenly she broke out into uncontrollable laughter, excitedly exclaiming, 'I am healed! My leg is healed!' She later claimed that at this time she did not consider herself to be a Christian.

Despite the success of Wigglesworth's healing meetings, opposition was mounting from both the strong national church and the medical profession. When his Swedish hosts approached the police for permission to hold an outdoor meeting in Stockholm's great park the following Whit-Sunday, it was refused. Although it was argued that there was no building large enough to accommodate the crowds, the police still refused, and even took Wigglesworth and Pethrus, the Stockholm pastor, into custody, suspecting them of some kind of chicanery or even fraud. Eventually the police relented when no case could be proved against the two men. They explained that there was only one reason why they refused permission for the open-air meeting: if Wigglesworth were to put his hand on the sick in their great park it would take thirty police officers to guard the situation. They did, however, give permission to use the park on condition that Wigglesworth did not lay hands upon the people.

Wigglesworth agreed to the request and arrangements for

the huge gathering in the park were made. 'When the presence of the Lord is there to heal,' commented Smith, 'it does not require the laying-on-of-hands. Faith is the great operating factor. When we believe God, all this is easy.'

A large platform was erected in the park to enable him to preach to the crowds. It was estimated they numbered over twenty thousand. But how was he to reach so many people in the way to which he was accustomed? As he stood on the platform gazing down on the sea of faces, he sent up one of his urgent prayers. 'Lord, you know the situation. You have never yet been in a fix where you could not handle the situation. Show me what can be done for this poor and needy people without having hands laid upon them. Show me.'

'Wholesale healings'

The answer to that prayer was to be the beginning of what he called 'wholesale healings' and 'retail healings'.

Wigglesworth preached with freedom and ease. He was keenly aware of the presence of the Holy Spirit upon him and of his leading in what he should do. At the conclusion of his message he said, 'All of you who would like the power of God to go through you today, healing everything, put your hands up.' As the thousands of hands were raised, Smith sent up another silent prayer to his master, 'O Lord show me.' Then he clearly heard God speak to him. He was instructed to ask for the person who was standing on a rock to keep his or her hand raised, when the others lowered theirs. In spite of knowing that there were many rocks in this park, he did as he was told. All hands were lowered except for one woman. He then said to the woman, 'Tell all the people what are your troubles.' She said that she was in so much pain that unless she sat down she would collapse.

Wigglesworth did not appear to take notice of this. Instead he told her to raise both her hands high. Then he shouted, 'In the name of Jesus, I rebuke the evil one, from your head to

your feet, and I believe God has loosened you.' The woman
felt a surge of power through her body and immediately
jumped and shouted with joy. She was the first to be healed
that day.

He then told all the sick people to place their hands on the
disease-affected parts of their bodies. 'Now each one lay
hands on yourself,' he added, 'and when I pray God will heal
you.' Hundreds of people were healed that day.

This encouraged Wigglesworth; after the meeting he said
to his Swedish colleagues that God 'revealed to me' for the
first time that it was a simple matter for Jesus to 'heal without
the laying on of my hands'.

The opposition to Wigglesworth's meetings were still not at
an end. The leaders of the Lutheran Church persisted in their
attempts to prevent him continuing his work in Sweden.
Supported by leading physicians, they appealed to the King
of Sweden to issue orders banning him from the country. But
one of the king's personal nursing staff, who herself had been
healed in one of Smith's meetings, told the king, 'I have been
so wonderfully healed by this man. You know I am walking
alright now.' 'Yes,' said the king, 'I know everything about
him. Tell him to go. I do not want him turned out. If he goes
now, he can come back. But if he is turned out he cannot
come back.'

Norway and Denmark

Norway and Denmark were the scenes of significant events in
this early part of Smith Wigglesworth's international
ministry.

In both the capital cities of Oslo and Copenhagen
thousands attended his daily meetings.

Thomas Barratt, who had brought the Pentecostal
message to Europe, was so impressed with Smith Wigglesworth's unique form of ministry that he invited him to
conduct services in his church in Oslo. He arrived a week

ahead of the Easter Convention and ministered three times on the preceding Sunday. The church building was able to accommodate two thousand, but this soon proved to be inadequate. In his report of the events, Barratt says, 'We really did not know what we should do to receive the extra crowds . . . There is no larger hall in the city except the large Lutheran hall, but they had stated that they would not let me have it unless I promised not to speak in tongues. And I, of course, could not make such a promise.'

The faith of the people was running at an all-time high. One hospital patient asked his doctor for permission to attend the meetings. The doctor said, 'If you go, you will not be allowed back.' In spite of this warning, he decided to go to the meeting hall because he believed it would be unnecessary to return. He was healed, and he threw his crutches away.

The ongoing blessings from Smith Wigglesworth's ministry in Norway were being experienced as far away as Chicago and Los Angeles, both at the time and even after his death.

For example, Stanley Frodsham, while on a preaching visit to Bethel Temple in Los Angeles, met a Norwegian who, in the mid-1920s, was dying from tuberculosis of the lungs. One lung had already collapsed. He told of his remarkable deliverance from this scourge of the day and of how subsequently he had decided to emigrate to North America. Not only had he been healed, but after a thorough examination by the USA immigration authorities he was accepted as medically fit even though there were strict regulations prevailing at the time.

Some years later this same man was living in Chicago when Smith Wigglesworth was there for a series of meetings. The Norwegian's wife was now the one in need of healing. She was also suffering from a disease of the lungs. 'Who better than Wigglesworth to pray for her?' thought her husband, and promptly arranged to take her to one of his meetings. Smith Wigglesworth prayed for her. She was not only healed, but though previously unable to bear children, now found herself pregnant. Not believing her to be healed, her doctor predicted the worse for mother and child. He was not only proved wrong, but a healthy baby was born with no ill-effects to the mother. The mother subsequently gave birth to a further two children, and all four were in the best of health at the time her husband told Frodsham this story.

16   Across the high seas

God moves in a mysterious way
His wonders to perform

In all probability these words often came to Wigglesworth's mind during his years of travelling ministry. They were certainly appropriate for his missions to Australia and New Zealand.

The year was 1921. Two men who were complete strangers to each other and who lived many thousands of miles apart, were destined to meet in Denmark. One was from a province in southwest China adjoining Burma and Vietnam. The other from a little-known street in Bradford, Yorkshire.

J Fullerton was a Danish missionary serving with the China Inland Mission. Two years earlier, in 1919, he was in the province of Yünnan when there was an outpouring of the Holy Spirit and Christians found themselves 'speaking in other tongues'. Fullerton, a godly man who spent much time in prayer, welcomed this experience. But, as was too often the case in those days, because of this he was dismissed by the CIM board. Undaunted, he moved north and launched his own mission base in Honan, a province in the central part of China. It covers an area of some sixty-five thousand square miles, and today has a population almost equal to the United Kingdom. He was remarkably successful, and it is a wonder not more is known of him. Some nine thousand Chinese, who had previously been worshipping idols, were added to the churches he established.

During one of his evening prayer times in his little chapel in Loyang he felt 'strangely moved' to pray for a country quite

unfamiliar to him, New Zealand. British missionaries had
been there for more than a hundred years, and many
immigrants had brought their Christian faith with them. In
addition there was a whole galaxy of eminent evangelical
preachers speaking at various prophetic conventions at this
time. New Zealand was not, by any stretch of the
imagination, short of sound biblical exposition, so the
burden Fullerton was experiencing for this country was
inexplicable.

On furlough during 1921, Fullerton returned to his home
country Denmark. 'Coincidentally' he returned when
Wigglesworth was conducting one of his missions in
Copenhagen. Fullerton and Wigglesworth met. Had Wigglesworth ever thought of going to New Zealand, was Fullerton's
question. Wigglesworth had not. The Danish missionary
then shared his strange burden with Smith, who promised to
make it a matter of earnest prayer.

Following his return from Scandinavia, Smith Wigglesworth waited upon the Lord for his directions. It did not take
long before he was convinced that he should go to New
Zealand and wrote of this to Fullerton, who made contact
with some Christian leaders in Wellington. They, in turn, set
up preliminary arrangements for an evangelistic crusade.

Coinciding with these events was an invitation to visit
Australia. This came from Mrs Janet Lancaster, who was the
leader of the Good News Hall in Melbourne. She even raised
the princely sum of £250, an average wage for a year in
those days, to pay for his sea passage. In the latter part of
1921 Wigglesworth set sail for Australia and New Zealand.

The entertainer

'I'm planning an evening's entertainment for the passengers,'
the ship's entertainment officer told Smith, soon after the
ship got under way. 'Would you like to be included in the
programme?' 'Certainly,' Smith replied. 'I'll do anything

that's helpful.' 'Then, what can you do?' asked the officer. 'Sing,' he said. 'Fine,' commented the officer, 'we could do with a singer', little realising what was to come. 'Have you any preference for the part of the programme when you will render your solo?' he asked, showing Smith a draft of it. Now Smith, with a mischievous thought, noticed that the highlight of the evening was the dance. 'Well, let's see,' he mused. Then pointing his finger to the place before the dance item he said, 'Put me down for that spot – just before the dance.' 'Certainly,' obliged the unwitting officer.

The evening for the entertainment duly arrived. Smith seated himself with the rest of the passengers and waited, somewhat impatiently, for his turn to come. Eventually the entertainment officer, who was also the compere for the evening, announced, 'Next we have a solo from Mr Wigglesworth from Yorkshire.'

Smith immediately walked to the piano and handed the pianist his copy of *Redemption Songs*, indicating the music of hymn number 809. As soon as she saw the words she was horrified and refused to accept it, saying she could not accompany him. Unabashed he turned and faced the audience, many of whom were in evening dress, and launched into his solo unaccompanied. With his fine baritone voice he sang:

If I could only tell Him as I know Him
My Redeemer who has brightened all my way.
If I could tell how precious is His presence,
I am sure that you would make Him yours today.

Then with great gusto, his voice filling the ship's salon, he entered the refrain:

Could I tell it? Could I tell it?
How the sunshine of His presence lights my way.
I would tell it, I would tell it,
And I'm sure you would make Him yours today.

The atmosphere was electric. If someone had struck a match the place would have exploded. But Smith was not finished. He launched into the second verse:

If I could tell you how He loves you,
And if we could through the lonely garden go.
If I could tell His dying pain and pardon,
You would worship at His wounded feet I know.

Eventually, he came to the last verse:

But I can never tell Him as I know Him,
Human tongue can never tell all love Divine.
I can only entreat you to accept Him,
You can know Him only when you make Him thine.

Then came the final refrain, 'Could I tell it?...' And with great emphasis he thundered out the answer, 'I would tell it... And I'm sure you would make Him yours today.'

When he finished his solo the audience could not proceed with the dance. 'You've spoiled it,' some complained. A clergyman going to India as a missionary pushed his way through the crowd and brusquely complained to Wigglesworth, 'How dare you sing that song?' 'How dare I not sing that song?' retorted Smith. 'It was my opportunity. How could I not tell it?'

Wigglesworth later heard that when the clergyman reached India he sent a report back to the London office of his society: 'I did not seem to have any opportunities to preach on board ship. But there was a plumber on board who seemed to have plenty of opportunity to preach to everybody. And he said things to me that I just can't get out of my mind. One thing he said that I can't forget, is that the Acts of the Apostles was only written because they acted.'

The morning after the concert Smith was the talking point of everyone on board. As he was taking his constitutional walk along the boat deck he was approached by a young couple. 'We're in a terrible state,' they said. 'We're looking after a gentleman and lady in the first class section. She is a Christian Scientist, one of their greatest teachers, and she has been taken seriously ill. And the ship's doctor gives little hope. We told her about you, and she says she would like to see you.'

Wigglesworth agreed to see the lady. He went to her cabin, and with his usual abruptness said, 'I'm not going to speak to you about anything. Not about your sickness, or anything. I am simply going to lay hands on you in the name of Jesus, and the moment I do, you will be healed.'

He thereupon placed his hands on the woman and commanded the sickness to leave her. She was immediately healed and rose from her bed. The effect on her was one of bewilderment. For three days she walked the decks greatly troubled. But Wigglesworth resisted the temptation to talk to her. He waited for the Holy Spirit to speak to her first. Feeling greatly puzzled she called for Smith to visit her once more.

'What shall I do?' she asked him. 'What do you mean?' he replied. 'For three years I have been preaching about Christian Science all over England. We live in a great house in India, and we have another large house in London. But now my life has been changed. This is the real thing. I'm a new woman.' She told him that she had a new joy, but then asked: 'Shall I be able to continue smoking cigarettes?' To her astonishment he said, 'Yes, of course you can. Smoke as many as you can. Smoke night and day, if you can.' Then she said, 'You know we play cards, bridge and other things. Can I continue to play?' 'Yes,' he replied. 'Play all night through. Go on playing if you can.' Finally, she said, 'You know, we have a little wine. Just a little wine with our friends, here in the first class. Is that alright? Or, shall I give it up?' 'No,' he told her. 'Drink all you want.' Again adding, 'If you can.'

The ship continued its journey through the Suez Canal and the Red Sea, and then stopped at Aden to refuel. By this time important changes had begun to take place in the woman's life. Wigglesworth had been wise enough to recognise that if he had ordered her to give up these so-called 'necessities' the change would be of his making, rather than that of the Holy Spirit.

On their arrival at Aden she instructed her maid to take a message to the ship's wireless officer. It was to cancel a consignment of cigarettes she had ordered before leaving London. 'My life has been changed. I cannot go along with all these things again,' was her explanation.

Pearl of the Indian Ocean

Sri Lanka, or Ceylon as it was then called, was affectionately described as the 'Pearl of the Indian Ocean'. Via the novelist Horace Walpole, Sri Lanka gave the word 'serendipity', meaning 'a happy chance', to the English language. It appears that he 'came upon this island by chance'.

It is a beautiful island (I once spent two happy years there), a place of jewels and gems, of golden sands and 'golden water' (which some mundanely call 'tea'), and sleepy, pineapple and coconut-clad, lagoons; a place of once-genteel people and mischievous monkeys.

During his voyage, Wigglesworth's ship called there. But his was not to be a sight-seeing trip. Those who knew he was coming so filled his four days with preaching and praying that he had little time for anything else. And the crowds besieged him. 'You know, four days is not much to give us,' they said. 'No,' he agreed, 'but it's a good share!'

As miracles of healing occurred so the numbers multiplied until there were six thousand attending the meetings in spite of a temperature of 110 degrees. And thousands more waited outside. The local leaders continued to plead. 'What are we going to do, because we are not touching the people at all?' 'Can you have a meeting early in the morning – at eight o'clock?' he asked. They said they would arrange it.

One of the Colombo newspapers reported: 'People have been known to have come from all parts of the island, including sick folk devoid of all hope and help. They had to wait for hours for the doors of the hall to be opened. The majority, if not all, went away sound in mind and body. As a testimony of the efficacy of prayer and the healing of sicknesses, Speldenwinder of Kandy, who suffered from a virulent cancer in the stomach, and whose case was abandoned as hopeless by scientific men, on Tuesday confessed to having been completely freed of the disease by Mr Wigglesworth's prayer. People of all sorts, of all ages, and classes, of diverse religions and professions, have attended Mr Wigglesworth's meetings, and though there have been scoffers among them, nearly all of them have gone away impressed by his words and actions... Considering the diversity of races and creeds in Ceylon, the numbers attached to this campaign may be said to constitute a record.'

The report also described various kinds of healings, including Wigglesworth's practice of praying over hand-kerchiefs belonging to sick people who could not attend the meetings. After prayer these were taken to the sick and placed on them with miraculous results.

This is what Wigglesworth had to say about those meetings when he reached Australia: 'I believe you need to have something more than smoke to touch people. You need to be a burning light for that. His ministers must be flames of fire. There were thousands outside to hear the Word of God. There were about three thousand people crying for mercy at once. I tell you it was a sight. But I tell you a flame of fire can do anything! Things can change in the fire. It was an experience of the people in the eleventh chapter of Hebrews. This is Pentecost! It must go UP. If ever it goes down it will never go up again. The prospects are so wonderful that you will say, LORD – HIGHER! What about your feet? Never mind them, get your head in the right place! And whatever you do, don't let your heart get in the wrong place, for it is there where all the illumination comes, and you are made a flame by the igniting of his power inside.

'It will come as sure as anything. But what moved me more than anything was this – and I say it this morning with thought and with a broken spirit, because I would not like to mislead you in any way. There were hundreds who tried to touch me. They were so impressed with the power of God that was present. They testified everywhere that with a touch they were healed. It was not the virtue of Wigglesworth. It was the same faith in the Son of God that was with those at Jerusalem when they said that Peter's shadow healed them.'

Australia

'I want you folks to know that I am going to prophesy in the name of the Lord that this woman is going to walk. If that prophecy does not come to pass, I will never prophesy again. But if it does come to pass, you will know that there is a prophet in the midst.' That was how Wigglesworth began his ministry in a Baptist church in Sydney, New South Wales.

In front of him was a woman confined to a wheelchair. On the platform was a medical doctor by the name of Fallon, a member of that church. It was on his recommendation that the minister, the Rev William Lamb, who was also on the platform, allowed Smith Wigglesworth to occupy the pulpit. The minister, however, was unaware that Wigglesworth was Pentecostal.

A certain Philip Duncan, describing the effect of Wigglesworth's opening statement, later said: 'All the deacons were looking at the minister. Dr Fallon was looking at his boots. And Wigglesworth was looking to the Lord.'

In the dramatic silence that followed, Wigglesworth prayed for the woman. The tension in the atmosphere was almost unbearable. Then, looking straight at the woman, he said, 'In the name of the Lord, be free!' He lifted the woman from the chair and told her to walk. She said she couldn't. So, as Barry Chant puts it in his book *Heart of Fire*: 'Wigglesworth told her that the Lord had healed her, and she could walk. To prove it, he pushed her in the middle of the back. She walked!'

After a period in Sydney, Wigglesworth continued on to Melbourne, the venue to which he had first been invited. He opened his Melbourne campaign in Mrs Lancaster's Good News Hall. People flocked there when they heard of the many conversions and healings. One of the more sensational healings was of a Mr Harrison, whose son later became the principal of the Commonwealth Bible College. He went forward for prayer. He had more than thirty cancerous lumps around his neck and, as a result, could not wear a collar or tie. Surgery was considered to be of no value. Wigglesworth prayed for him, then said, 'Go home and sleep. In the morning take off your bandage.' Then he hit the man on the neck and demanded in the name of his Lord that the growths would go. And they did! The next morning there was no trace of them.

News of this and similar healings spread through Melbourne like a prairie fire and the Good News Hall became too small to accommodate the crowds who came to see Wigglesworth. The meetings were then transferred to the huge Wirth's Olympia. This was the headquarters of the circus by that name.

The wording of this advertisement, which appeared in one of Melbourne's newspapers, carries the mark of either the evangelist's audacity or his faith:

THE DEAF HEAR – THE DUMB SPEAK
The deaf hear, the dumb speak, the lame walk, the paralytic gets out of his chair and pushes
WONDERFUL MIRACLES ARE BEING SEEN AT THE OLYMPIA

When the Yorkshire evangelist Smith Wigglesworth prayed for Mrs Johnson of Springvale, who had been in a chair for over six years, she got out and walked about the building and to the railway station having no more use for the chair

The platform in the Olympia was about eight feet high, and one evening Smith was more 'mobile' than ever. As his sermon unfolded, so he got closer and closer to the edge of the platform. At the height of his fervour the inevitable happened. He went perilously close to the edge, swayed to and fro for a few seconds trying to regain his balance. His arms flailing, Wigglesworth fell to the floor, and, still swaying somewhat, he surprisingly managed to land on his feet, whereupon he staggered up the aisle, his arms swinging like windmill sails, in a last-ditch effort to maintain his balance. All the while, he managed to keep preaching without so much as a pause. In a last desperate attempt to remain upright, he placed his hand on the shoulder of a man seated on one side of the aisle. At the close of the meeting the man came forward, excitedly explaining that the pain in his body for which he was going to ask for prayer had left him immediately Smith Wigglesworth's hand rested on his shoulder.

It was estimated that altogether one thousand people professed conversions during this series of meetings.

From Melbourne he moved on to Adelaide where, though not as numerically successful, the nucleus of the Pentecostal work in South Australia was formed. This arose out of the healing of a man, due for hospital treatment the next day, who was suffering from a badly poisoned hand. As Wigglesworth came to him in the healing line, he asked him what his trouble was. The young man told him. Smith said, 'That's alright, sonny. The Lord knows all about that. Put your trust in the Lord. You'll be alright.'

Praying for others, Wigglesworth moved along the line. A few minutes later he was back and said, 'Hey, sonny, take those bandages off.' He did. There was no swelling, no mark, and no need of a hospital.

Even to the 'Aussies' Wigglesworth was unorthodox. Janet Lancaster's son-in-law, W A Buchanan, who later became a well-known leader in the Christian book trade, travelled with

Wigglesworth on his tour and sometimes shared the same overnight accommodation. He related some of the trip's more humorous happenings to his son Clarry. 'It was particularly noticeable,' wrote Clarry, 'that when ready to retire "Wiggy" (as our family affectionately called him), donned in his old-fashioned night shirt would jump into the middle of the bed uttering the words "Good-night, Lord." And would be asleep immediately.' Buchanan's explanation was that as Smith literally walked and talked with the Lord throughout the day, he had no need to wait for an audience before retiring.

New Zealand

There is no doubt that of all the places Smith Wigglesworth was destined to visit, New Zealand was unique.

The Danish missionary Fullerton and his wife had planned their return to China to take them via New Zealand so as to coincide with the arrival of Wigglesworth, but this was not to be. Wigglesworth was delayed in Australia, and the Fullertons had to continue on their way to China. However, this missionary had fulfilled his part in what he believed to be God's plan for New Zealand, and that plan included Smith Wigglesworth.

The Buchanans were now Wigglesworth's helpers and went ahead to Wellington in order to make the necessary arrangements. But with very limited financial resources little could be done by way of advertising to make his coming known. The only announcements that could be made, were done by a small group called the Christian Covenanters Society.

It was late May 1922 before Smith Wigglesworth reached Wellington. Hardly anyone knew of him or of what had happened during his meetings in Ceylon and Australia, so his opening engagement was in a small Sunday school hall adjoining the Vivian Street Baptist Church.

In these unpretentious circumstances he met with relatively small congregations. Two daily services were held, one in the morning and the other in the evening. No one at this time could have believed that this would be the birthplace of today's Pentecostal movement in New Zealand.

For the morning meetings Wigglesworth concentrated his ministry on Bible studies. The subjects were mainly related to the work of the Holy Spirit, especially the Spirit's enduement of power and gifts for the edification and advancement of the church. His sermon titles during these early meetings reveal his intentions: Faith, The Baptism of the Holy Spirit, The Gifts of the Holy Spirit, The Sanctification of the Believer, The Second Coming of Christ, Divine Healing of the Sick, Exorcism of Evil Spirits.

The evening meetings included prayers for the sick. A comatose woman, who was at an advanced stage of tuberculosis, was carried into the hall on a stretcher. In his customary forthright and fearless manner, Smith commanded her sickness to leave. Instantly the woman sat up on the stretcher. Then, as the astonished congregation looked on, she stood up and walked around the hall. When it dawned on the people what they were witnessing – a modern-day miracle – the place erupted into sounds of uncontrollable excitement.

News of this and other healings spread through the city. The Sunday school hall became too small and the meetings had to be transferred to the main church. This again was filled with numbers reaching eight hundred. Then it was the turn of the Town Hall, where numbers quickly jumped to three thousand. In spite of this, many were left outside, unable to get in due to lack of space. Not only were people being converted and healed, some in a sensational manner, but many others were being baptised in the Spirit. Wigglesworth continued his preaching and praying without adjusting his methods one iota. To the consternation of newcomers to his meetings he would intersperse his sermons with utterances in tongues, then give the interpretation.

On May 31st the *Dominion*, Wellington's daily newspaper, carried a lengthy report of the Town Hall meetings under the banner headlines. 'Faith healing. Extraordinary scenes at Town Hall. The deaf made to hear.' E E Pennington, who was chairman of the New Zealand Evangelical Mission, reported: 'Evangelist Wigglesworth came to Wellington, little known to any of us. There was no flourishing of trumpets to herald this event. A few small advertisements in the local Press announced his meetings... His message was truly wonderful. If ever it could be said of a preacher of righteousness since the days of Phillip that he preached Christ unto them, it surely would apply to Brother Wigglesworth. Never has the writer witnessed such scenes that followed the presentation of the word of God by this Spirit-filled man, although he has been associated with such mighty evangelical services as those of Drs Torrey, Henry Chapman and others in their New Zealand Campaign. In the Wigglesworth services sometimes 400–500 responded in a meeting with whole families entering the kingdom of God.'

H V Roberts, in his book *New Zealand's Greatest Revival*, relates the story of a Salvation Army officer from Brisbane who, with about a thousand other people, could not gain admission to one of the Town Hall meetings. In spite of the fact that he had come such a distance, his protestations were in vain. There just was not a single seat or standing space for him. However, he turned it to good account by preaching to those outside, resulting in twenty conversions.

Wigglesworth then moved on to Christchurch at the invitation of the Sydenham Gospel Mission. They had welcomed the Pentecostal teaching and blessings two years earlier.

This time the advertising was on a larger scale. Prominently displayed in the Press adverts was the question, 'Have you been endued with power from on high?' This served to attract many Christians dissatisfied with their sterile church life, as well as the curious outsider. Again, capacity crowds attended the meetings, filling the halls; again, just as many failed to gain admittance. But now, with the increasing success of Wigglesworth's meetings, the Press reporting became snide and eventually very critical.

The editor of the *Sun* used his columns to pour scorn on Wigglesworth personally, as well as on his teachings. He was criticised for his accent, and, of course, for his methods. He was described as 'a man of rather unusual physical and oratorical vigour' who 'first worked up [the audience] into a condition of religious ecstasy'. His offer of healing to 'an incurable with the certainty of cure, when there can be no chance of success' was branded as 'the cruellest kind of torture'. 'When,' continued the report, 'the blind person he has treated is unable to see – the fault is the patient's, not his. "You haven't enough faith," he tells a shrinking sufferer.' The report asserted dismissively, 'He is just an ordinary faith-healer, with a knowledge of mob psychology and possibly a measure of magnetism above the average.' Then, revealing more about himself than Wigglesworth, the writer concluded, 'The age of miracles is past.'

In spite of the bad press, which those who were healed did not allow to go unchallenged, the campaign meetings, with their conversions, baptisms and healings, continued to attract larger and larger numbers of people. These included, according to a favourable newspaper item, 'men in business in our city, and among them I saw respected and prosperous businessmen'.

After Christchurch Wigglesworth went south to Dunedin, using the Early Settlers' Hall for his weekday services and the Burns Hall for Sundays. Here the enthusiasm of the crowds was so great that those unable to gain admission climbed the outside walls to the top windows to get a view of him.

Hundreds continued to be turned away, so the campaign sponsors hired the vast Princess Theatre. The large numbers of Dunedin's inhabitants wishing to attend Wigglesworth's meetings could not be explained away by arguing there was a scarcity of religious meetings in the city. In fact, the Saturday night editions of Dunedin's *Evening Star* carried advertisements for some forty-eight different church services. However, here again the Press decided to attack Wigglesworth, though one reporter, describing a case of exorcism in the paper's columns of June 15th 1922, had to admit, 'When the evangelist realised that, from the substance of the supplication, the evil spirit had got a firm hold, he would exhort Satan in almost fierce tones to "Come out", and as far as the reporter could see, the spirit did depart and depart swiftly (there was no waste of time), each case occupying but a few seconds, and the deaf heard and the dumb spoke.'

Wigglesworth continued at Dunedin until the end of June, and with barely time for travel was back in Wellington to begin his second campaign in the city on July 2nd.

With the recent experience of the large numbers attending the meetings, the local organisers decided to book the Town Hall for the Sunday meetings and the Taranaki Street Methodist Church for weeknights. Although the latter seated twelve hundred many were still unable to get seats. Such was the congestion inside the church that police had to be present to enable Wigglesworth to get to the pulpit.

Miraculous healings were the order of the day, as well as scores of Christians being baptised in the Spirit. The elderly caretaker of the Methodist Church said the scenes around him were reminiscent of the London Methodists of his youth who would pound the chairs and shout their prayers in raucous style. Unbelievers in the meetings would clamber over chairs and forms to get to the altar to pray.

Once again the Press raised a hue and cry as they sought to hound Wigglesworth, with the result that some of Wellington's prominent Christian leaders arranged for a number of affidavits to be drawn up by people who testified to having been healed. These were signed in the presence of a well-known and highly respected Justice of the Peace, C A Baker. They were subsequently examined by a journalist on the staff of the *Dominion*, who wrote in his report, 'The affidavits are genuine... The first is that of a dairyman who suffered from chronic gastritis and paralysis of both legs from the hips downwards, and could only drag his legs along with crutches. After prayer he did not need the crutches and walked home.'

He then told of the plight of a twenty-one year old woman who had suffered from double curvature of the spine for the whole of her life. She could not rise from the floor without pulling herself up with both hands. One leg was measured and found to be three inches shorter than the other. Wigglesworth laid hands on her, prayed, commanded her to stand, then walk. And she did. The previously cynical reporter wrote: 'Her spine straightened, her leg lengthened, and her diseased hip was healed. The following Sunday she was able to walk several miles to and from the meetings.' He concluded, 'There are several other affidavits of a similar nature but space will not permit of their publication.'

Smith continued his practice of praying over handkerchiefs brought from the sick who were unable to attend in person. The extent of this part of his ministry can be seen in an announcement in the Press at the close of these meetings to the effect that a thousand handkerchiefs were still awaiting collection.

A few days after the conclusion of this second crusade, the committee responsible for arranging Wigglesworth's meetings decided to disband. They considered their work finished.

However, by this time there were many prayer meetings taking place throughout the environs of Wellington as a direct result of the Wigglesworth crusade. To co-ordinate these meetings, a committee of six men was formed. The meetings continued to grow spontaneously. So, the committee deemed it necessary to give a name to this emerging organisation. It was called, 'Wellington City Mission', and this was the beginning of the Pentecostal Church in New Zealand.

James Worsfold, in his interesting and well-documented book, *A History of the Charismatic Movements in New Zealand*, writes: 'At the conclusion of the Wellington services the Evangelist [Wigglesworth] left New Zealand for further crusades, but already the committee had minuted the express desire of the congregations to invite the Evangelist to return to New Zealand. This he did in 1923. While there is no specific evidence that any special efforts were put forth by the leaders to create a new organisation, one was actually being born, for many who had experienced conversion, divine healing, sanctification and the baptism in the Holy Spirit with the accompanying sign of glossolalia [tongues] were meeting with antagonism, sad to say, from fellow members of their churches, and in some cases, their ministers. This, as usual, only served to weld them together, and the Evangelist had already conducted a Breaking of Bread service in the Paramount Theatre on Sunday at 11 am. This to many must have appeared significant.'

In addition to the central meetings held in the centre of the capital city, the leaders soon had to arrange for services in more convenient places around Wellington. On Sundays there was a choice of three morning services and three Sunday schools and two evening services. With the exception of Monday, there were meetings in different parts of the city every night of the week.

New Zealand's second visit

Smith Wigglesworth returned to New Zealand in October 1923 and conducted successful crusades in Auckland, Palmerston North, Blenheim and finally Wellington.

In spite of the signed affidavits which the newspapers had published the previous year, he again received a mixed reception from the Press. His unusual way of praying seemed to get in the way of their believing. A Blenheim pressman reported, 'His method is remarkable for he stands on no ceremony. With coat removed he laid hands very violently indeed on the afflicted parts of the various people's anatomy while he called, in stentorian tones, on evil spirits possessing them to come out. And in one case dealt a frail old lady such a smack in the stomach as might well have doubled her up. His patients, however, stood up unflinchingly to his assaults, and in every case declared themselves improved in health by the encounter.

'There was one case which was rather remarkable. It was that of a woman who had been suffering for three years with a bad leg and other ailments. She hobbled before the missioner on a stick, but before he had finished with her she was able to walk erect and to run agilely enough up and down the hall.'

This was to be Wigglesworth's last crusade in Blenheim and on December 16th he crossed Cook Strait to Wellington where he ministered at the first Pentecostal Convention to be held in New Zealand. This lasted from December 23rd to 30th, and was followed by his fourth and final evangelistic and healing crusade for which he could spare only two weeks.

One of the stories Wigglesworth used to tell of the New Zealand meetings was of a very large and well-built woman. Due to her size he could not help noticing her in the healing line. 'God revealed to me the presence of the enemy in her body,' he said. Dealing with her in his usual manner he commanded the demons to leave her. 'You are killing me,' she cried out as she fell in the middle of the aisle. 'Lift her up,' Smith told the ushers. 'God hasn't finished with her yet.' She was delivered of the evil power and a cancerous growth in her body. When telling this story on his arrival in North America, his next port of call, he added: 'It is wise to believe God. God has a place for the man or woman who dares to believe him. The man God has his hand on is not subject to the opinion of others. This our father Abraham found pertaining to the flesh. May God increase the number who dare to believe in all circumstances.'

Before Wigglesworth left New Zealand a denominational organisation had begun to form, but he would have no part of it, declining to attend any executive or administrative committee meetings. This was his attitude to all conferences dealing with church administration. He also refused to become a registered member of any religious denomination or movement. Many thought him to be a member of the

Assemblies of God, because he more often than not worked with them, but he remained independent.

Wigglesworth did not return again to New Zealand, although he was contemplating a visit in response to a pressing invitation from the churches following the end of the Second World War. During May 1972 the New Zealand Pentecostal churches held commemorative services at which the late Percy S Brewster of Great Britain was the guest speaker. This was fifty years from the first visit of Smith Wigglesworth, which now marks the beginning of the Pentecostal movement in that country.

17 Mission America

From New Zealand Smith Wigglesworth journeyed on to Canada and the United States. He was to enjoy many such visits and there are still memories of his meetings recounted by those who were there at the time.

Conquering the devil

Ruth Steelberg Carter has already been quoted. During my American visit in connection with this book I heard her talk of the day, when married to the late Wesley Steelberg, she entertained Smith in her home. She gave her impressions of what it was like to sit under his ministry in the Oakland Assemblies of God Church, which her then husband pastored.

'I first met him in 1924 when he came to a camp meeting in Berkeley, California, as a speaker. He was a very rugged man. He said the reason why he was so rough was that he was fighting the devil, not the person. The sickness that was in that person. He believed that the devil had to be dealt with severely.

'He was also a man of the Spirit. I remember him once at our home and we were sitting at the dinner table after our meal. The men present were telling amusing incidents from their past. And we were having a real good time of fellowship. And Brother Wigglesworth was entering right into it all. Then all of a sudden he said, "It's enough." He got up from the table and not another word was said. He had got a little caution in his spirit that the conversation was getting out of hand, a little too light. And that was it.'

During this time when Smith was with the Steelbergs, a friend of theirs by the name of Craig, the pastor of the Glad Tidings Assembly of San Francisco, visited their home. He was suffering from a stiff neck. 'And I can see him yet,' recalled Ruth, 'coming up the stairs with his head on one side. It hurt just to move that neck.' Wigglesworth barked at him. 'What's up with you?' 'My neck. I have a stiff neck,' he replied. As Craig reached the top of the stairs, Wigglesworth confronted him. He took hold of Craig's head in his huge hands and as he demanded healing 'in the name of Jesus', rolled his head around repeatedly. Apparently this pastor went staggering back down the steps holding his head, but he was healed.

When challenged about his roughness, he compared the way he approached the devil with the lady who was persistently followed by her dog. In spite of her repeated orders to the dog in gentle tones to return home, the dog refused to obey. But then she got angry and screamed at the dog in desperation, 'Go home.' It did.

He once prayed for a man who had cancer of the rectum. Night and day morphia was administered to him to alleviate the pain. Wigglesworth prayed for him and he was healed. Most significantly, when he was relating this incident on his return to England, he said, 'The Spirit of God came upon me. In the name of Jesus, I laid hold of the evil power with hatred in my heart against the powers of Satan.'

Wigglesworth constantly reminded his hearers, 'Fear looks; faith jumps.' And jump he did, sometimes forcing others to jump as well. Jean Stone Wilson, in her book *Green Apples*, tells us of the young man Smith encountered outside the American church where he had been preaching. The young man was weeping. In response to Smith's question, 'What's hup, lad?' he said that he had been seeking the baptism in the Spirit but Jesus had not given it to him. 'Oh is

that all you want?', he said. Then he prayed, 'Lord, fill him
with the Holy Spirit,' and promptly struck him on the head.
The young man immediately burst out speaking in tongues.

En route from New Zealand to Vancouver, where he
commenced this tour of North America, the ship had called at
the Fiji islands. On board was a wealthy Canadian who was a
breeder of racehorses. When at Fiji this man was bitten by a
snake. 'He came on the ship, and his face was the picture of
death,' said Smith. 'He pulled his trousers up, and showed me
where the snake had bitten him. His leg was swollen.' The
frightened man kept repeating, 'I'm dying. I'm dying. Help
me.'

Giving this story in Canada he said, 'Oh the Book. The
Book. The Book. I could help him because in the Book there
is grace and plenty to spare. I would tonight that we drank in
this word, "I will give him power to bind and power to loose."
It is here, it is the Word of God. And in the name of Jesus,
placing my hand on his leg, I rebuked the devourer and cast it
out. He stamped his leg and said to me, "I am healed". He
pulled his trouser leg up again and there was the leg perfectly
healed, and the swelling gone down.

'We must not measure ourselves by ourselves. If we do we
shall always be small. Measure yourself by the will of God,
the great measurement that God brings to you. Don't be
fearful. He wants to make us strong, powerful, stalwart,
resolute, resting upon the authority of God.'

Tenderness and severity

Wigglesworth was, however, aware of the fear that made
many people hesitate to accept their healing, especially, as in
the following case, when the person had never known the
experience of walking, which most of us take for granted.

A man by the name of James Taylor witnessed at close
range a healing, the memory of which remained with him for
the rest of his life. He was seated in the second row 'almost

within hand reach of the healing corner' of the hall where
Wigglesworth was ministering. This was in Washington DC.
As he sat there he noticed a badly crippled young lady being
helped to the front row. 'Her legs absolutely dangled, with her
feet hanging vertically from them,' he later wrote to a friend.
'From her waist she seemed to be limp and powerless.'

Wigglesworth always gave priority to the gospel message in
his meetings, saying he would rather see one soul won for
Christ than a thousand healed, so it was after he gave his
gospel message that he invited those wishing to receive Christ
to come forward. As the enquirers began to move forward
this young lady also tried to come up. Seeing her attempt to
leave her seat, and recognising that she could not do so, he
said, 'Don't you worry my girl. You stay right where you are.
You're going to be a different girl when you leave this place.'

He proceeded with his instructions to the new converts,
prayed for them, and began his healing ministry. After he had
prayed for everyone who was sick, he returned to the girl. He
bent down and tenderly asked her to tell him her name. Then
he invited her to tell him the nature of her trouble. After she
did so, he stood up and addressed the congregation. 'This girl
has no muscles in her legs. She has never walked before. We
will pray for her.' Then, putting his hands on her head, he
cried out in a loud voice, 'In the name of Jesus Christ, walk!'
But the girl didn't move. He looked down at this pathetic
child and whispered to her, 'You are afraid, aren't you?' 'Yes,'
she said, somewhat timidly. 'There's no need to be,' he
assured her.

Then Wigglesworth, looking down on this young figure
before him, shouted, with no uncertain sound, 'You are
healed. Walk! Walk!' And she did. 'Slow steps at first,' wrote
Taylor. 'Just like a baby learning to walk for the first time.
Twice she walked in that way along the length of the
platform. When we left the hall we saw her crutches lying in
the seat. On reaching the sidewalk outside we saw her
standing as others do, talking with two girl friends.'

As tender as he was to the young girl, Smith could also be

severe to the proud. Once he went to the home of a woman who, he was told, had been suffering for many years. Her body was twisted up with rheumatism. He asked her, 'What makes you lie there?' 'It's my thorn in the flesh,' she replied. He promptly responded, 'To what wonderful degree of righteousness have you attained that you have to have a thorn in the flesh?' 'You don't understand,' she countered. 'I believe it is the Lord who is causing me to suffer.' Dismissing this as nonsense, he told the woman. 'You believe it is the Lord's will for you to suffer, and you are trying to get out of it as quickly as possible. There are doctor's bottles all over the place. Get out of your hiding place, and confess you are a sinner. If you will get out of your self-righteousness God will do something for you. Drop the idea that you are so holy that God has to afflict you. Sin is the cause of your sickness not righteousness.' And with that he left the house.

The late Stanley Frodsham was a regular travelling companion and personal friend of Smith Wigglesworth. He related the story of how, in an American city that must be nameless, Smith was 'pressed upon day after day' to go to the home of a wealthy lady member of his church who had donated large sums of money for the building of the hall where the meetings were taking place. She was said to be too ill to attend the service.

'We drew up at the door,' wrote Frodsham, 'rang the bell, and were ushered into a palatial room. From there we moved into a very large bedroom. There, like an eastern monarch on a throne, sat the gorgeously robed lady in a rainbow-coloured pile of lovely embroidered cushions.

'Smith Wigglesworth stood and stared at such a sight. Then he said, "Well! You certainly look comfortable!" "I beg your pardon," she snapped. "I said, 'You look very comfortable!'" She let loose a storm of abuse which left her exhausted. "Oh!" he said. "I can see that you are not ready for me yet. Good evening." And so saying he walked out of the house and entered the waiting automobile.'

'My wife and I,' continued Frodsham, 'followed him out

and ventured to suggest that he had been a bit harsh with the lady.' Much as he respected his friend Stanley's counsel, he briefly replied, 'I know my business.'

The pastor and his two associates remained with the lady to console her, but Wigglesworth was adamant that she was not ready for his prayers, and they left for the evening meeting.

The next morning the first of the thrice-daily services took place as usual. But this time they did not have the 'usual' end. At the close Wigglesworth gave his invitation to those who wished to come nearer to God: 'If you move forward only a foot, you will be blessed; if you move forward a yard, you will get more. If you come up to the platform we will pray for you, and God will meet your needs with his supply.'

Scores of people started to move forward. But this time they were led by a stately lady. She wanted to be first in line. But in her hurry she tripped and fell spreadeagled in front of Wigglesworth. He prayed for her, and she was instantly healed. She was the 'gorgeously-robed lady' of the 'rainbow-coloured cushions'.

As Frodsham wrote in his biography *Smith Wigglesworth, apostle of faith*, Wigglesworth did not distinguish between the colour of one's skin or the size of one's bank balance, and he held no truck with those who used either for their advantage.

Wigglesworth was fond of saying, 'There are two things that you must have in Pentecostal meetings. You must have an offering. And you must have a broken spirit,' and adding that you should not be ashamed of either. 'The nearer I get to God the more broken I am in spirit.'

Back from death's door

Although there is no complete record of Smith Wigglesworth's many and varied ministerial activities in North America, there are still many people alive to testify to the spiritual and physical benefits they received during his visits.

Travelling by car the day before writing these lines, I found myself spiritually invigorated after listening on my cassette player to a taped testimony of a Los Angeles woman, Eve Alderman, sent to me by Faith Campbell, Stanley Frodsham's daughter.

Mrs Alderman was brought back to life from death's door during a Wigglesworth meeting in Los Angeles in 1925. Her doctors had pronounced her beyond hope. She was drifting in and out of a coma. Her body was like a skin-covered skeleton of little more than five stone in weight. But one day her husband carried her to a Wigglesworth meeting at which there were so many other sick people seeking healing he merely touched her and prayed the briefest of prayers. But she walked home. The next morning she rose from her bed like the rest of her family, and as the weeks passed her strength increased. It is probable that Wigglesworth never knew of the miracle that had occurred to Eve Alderman. But she lives today, and has a good strong voice on her recording.

During this trip, he went to Arizona which, at that time, was a 'sanatorium city' for TB sufferers, thousands of whom flocked to this desert country to 'take the cure'. Rich and poor alike, they came to Smith's meetings in their hundreds. They all had one thing in common – their lung trouble. There were so many he could not pray for them individually so his Swedish 'wholesale' healing was again put into operation. His task was to inspire faith first. Sometimes he did this by selecting one individual from the congregation. In one of these meetings he called out to a young lady who was in an advanced tubercular condition to leave her seat and stand in the nearest aisle. Breathing heavily and with cheeks flushed, she slowly did as she was told. 'I am going to pray for you, and then you will run around this building,' he told her. He prayed, then shouted 'Run.' But she didn't move. 'I can't run,' she said. 'I can scarcely stand.' 'Don't talk back to me,' was his brusque reply. 'Do as I have said.' Then he jumped down from the platform and put his arm around her and together they started to walk, then run and finally were jogging around the auditorium.

Audacious demonstration

Wigglesworth's son-in-law, James Salter, who had been a pioneer missionary in Africa, was also a man of great faith. Though he was Smith's constant companion for many years, sometimes even he would find himself fearful of Smith's bold announcements. 'He would often startle us in a meeting by saying, "Just to let you see that the Lord is in our midst and his power is present to heal and to bless, we are going to have an exhibition, a demonstration. In the Acts of the Apostles we read of 'All that Jesus began to do and to teach.' His 'doing' preceded his teaching. Every sermon Christ preached was prefaced by a model miracle. We are going to follow his example. The first person in this large audience who stands up, whatever his or her sickness, I'll pray for that one and God will deliver him or her."'

Salter told of one occasion when Wigglesworth made such an announcement. Large numbers of crippled people – some in wheelchairs, some lying on folding beds, – and twisted, pitiful cases of all kinds of diseases were in the audience. 'Secretly we have hoped that one of the simple cases would stand, and not one of the far-gone cancer cases or deformed cripples,' confessed Salter. But that 'secret' prayer wasn't always answered. A deformed man, with two sticks for support, struggled to his feet. In James Salter's own words, this is what followed: 'When Brother Wigglesworth saw him, he did not turn a hair. In his characteristic manner he asked, "Now, you: what's up with you?" After he had taken stock of the situation, he said, "All right, we will pray for you." He had the whole assembly join with him in prayer, and then, addressing the man, he said, "Now, put down your sticks and walk to me." The man fumbled for a time; then he let his sticks fall to the ground and began to shuffle along. "Walk! walk!" Brother Wigglesworth called, and the man stepped out. "Now run," he commanded, and the man did so to the amazement and great joy of all who were present, and to our unbounded relief!'

The discerning of spirits

Smith Wigglesworth exercised the gift of discernment of spirits in the face of much criticism, some of which came from fellow ministers. In one of his Los Angeles tent meetings a woman fainted, causing a disruption of the meeting. He treated this as the work of an evil spirit within her. Addressing himself to the prostrate figure, he said, 'I rebuke you, you devil, for disturbing this meeting.' The woman became quiet. But some of the congregation were incensed. They objected to what they thought of as his harshness to the woman.

Some days later, however, the woman's husband sought out Wigglesworth. Thanking him for the spiritual deliverance he had given his wife and the subsequent change, he said, 'Everything is different since the night you rebuked that evil power in her ... Doubtless she has been oppressed by a spirit of infirmity, but since you rebuked it the other night when she fainted, the thing has gone and now she is perfectly free.'

When in Kansas City Wigglesworth had to deal with a demon-possessed violent woman. He commanded the demon to leave her, then began to leave. The woman continued to follow him, pouring out vile curses on him. He turned around, and addressing himself to the demon in the woman said, 'I told you to leave.' And the woman was delivered.

The most important mission

Smith Wigglesworth visited the United States and Canada on many occasions, and many stories are recounted of the miraculous scenes that accompanied his ministry. Meetings were arranged for him in the major cities and they were always supported by capacity crowds. He was described as an evangelist, and rightly so because thousands of people were converted to Christ. He has also been called an apostle. Again, rightly so. He established churches and signs and wonders accompanied his ministry. But how did he see himself? Leslie Wigglesworth has no doubt about the answer. Repeatedly he told his grandson, 'My first and most important mission to every church is to stir up the people's faith in God.' As Stanley Frodsham described him, he was an 'Apostle of Faith'; literally, 'A messenger of faith in God'.

18 A way with words

One of the distinctive things about Smith Wigglesworth – and
it is something that most of his friends remember with a smile
– was his curious use of language. It will be remembered that
before his marriage to Polly he could neither read nor write.
But even though she managed to teach him to do both, he was
always hopeless at spelling. This may go some way to
explaining why he would often 'manufacture' his own words.

Wigglesworth's habit of coining non-dictionary words was
one of two things that singled him out from other preachers –
the other being the way he would intersperse his sermons with
'speaking in tongues', immediately followed by his own
interpretation. When asked by Rev George Stormont, then of
Leigh-on-Sea, why he felt it necessary to make up words, he
replied with a question, 'Do you ever have difficulty in
understanding what I mean?' George had to say, 'No'. 'That's
alright then, isn't it?' countered Smith with such finality in the
tone of his voice that there appeared to be no answer.

An unexpected ally?

I wonder if any of Wigglesworth's friends told him about the
philosopher, Wittgenstein? Perhaps the two 'W's' have now
met, and with a few wry smiles, have swopped notes on
Smith's 'word-making techniques'.

It was Wittgenstein who advanced the proposition that the
real meaning of words is always related to how they are
used. Wittgenstein was not worried about dictionary
definitions. They could be, at times, even misleading. So to be
sure of an individual's 'way with words' you need to see it or,

in Wigglesworth's case, hear it, in context. Would that have been a welcome imprimatur? If so, Smith had a distinguished ally without knowing it.

As I draw this life story of Smith Wigglesworth to a close, I offer some of his words as an insight into what that great man thought on issues that were to him of eternal worth.

Wigglesworth never wrote a book, although books have been written about him. However, one book was published bearing his name as author, *Ever-Increasing Faith*, being a collection of his sermons. He gave permission for this to be done, and the royalties were donated to Christian missions in Zaire. They were his public addresses recorded by shorthand writers and later transcribed (as were the extracts that follow).

Having read these remarkable results of his life of faith, you may be asking yourself a question countless others have asked: 'What was the secret of Wigglesworth's power?'

Speaking to members of Glad Tidings Assembly and Bible School in San Francisco soon after his sensational preaching and healing ministry in Scandinavia, he gave his personal account of the demonstration of God's power. I have used much of it earlier in the book. But he also added these words: 'I believe that there is only one way to all the treasures of God, and it is by the way of faith. There is only one principle underlying all the attributes and all the beatitudes of the mighty into the glories of Christ, and it is by faith... If you climb up any other way, you cannot work it out... You can have zeal without faith.'

Faith

To lend emphasis to this last statement he gave this original commentary on the apostle Peter's deliverance from prison: 'As I look into the twelfth chapter of Acts, I find that the people were praying all night for Peter to come out of prison. They had a zeal but seem to have been lacking in faith.

'They were to be commended for their zeal in spending their time in prayer without ceasing, but their faith, evidently, did not measure up to such a marvellous answer. Rhoda had more faith than the rest of them. When the knock came to the door, she ran to it, and the moment she heard Peter's voice, she ran back again with joy saying that Peter stood before the gate. And all the people said, "You're mad. It isn't so." But she constantly affirmed that it was even so.'

Answering his own question: 'How can you enter into a life of faith?' he said: 'All lack of faith is due to not feeding on God's Word. You need it every day. Feed on the living Christ of whom this Word is full. As you get taken up with the glorious fact and the wondrous presence of the living Christ, the faith of God will spring up within you. If I am going to know God, I am going to know him by his Word. I know I shall be in heaven, but I could not build on my feelings that I am going to heaven. I am going to heaven because God's Word says it, and I believe God's Word. "Faith cometh by hearing and hearing by the Word of God."'

Following that with this question: 'How shall we reach this *plane* of faith?' he had this to say: 'Let go your own thoughts, and take the thoughts of God, the Word of God. If you build yourself on imaginations you will go wrong. You have the Word of God and it is enough.'

Today the current theme of many preachers is 'positive thinking'. This is an area of quicksand and can be dangerous if it is not built on a 'positive foundation'. Emile Coué, the French psychotherapist and philosopher of the nineteenth century, who formulated the oft-repeated phrase, 'Every day and in every way, I am getting better and better,' is said to have died of a broken heart because no one believed him!

Faith's foundation

It was appropriate that Wigglesworth should speak of a solid foundation in a place like San Francisco, a city frighteningly vulnerable to earthquakes: 'Now beloved, you will clearly see this morning that God wants to bring us to a foundation. If we are ever going to make any progress in divine life we shall have to have a real foundation. And there is no foundation other than the foundation of faith for us...'

To follow Wigglesworth's thoughts here, I suggest you slow down your reading rate for the next few words: 'God is an inward witness of a power, of a truth, of a revelation, of an inward presence, of a divine knowledge. He is! He is! Then I must understand. I must clearly understand. I must have a basis of knowledge for everything that I say. We must, as preachers, never preach what we *think*. We must say what we *know*. Any man can think. You must be beyond the thinking. You must be in the teaching.'

To illustrate the importance of a solid foundation he would tell of his tram ride along the Lancashire seaboard. From the seaport of cosmopolitan Liverpool the tram would travel along Lancashire's coastline to the gusty resort of Blackpool. Along the way, Wigglesworth pointed out to his companion the folly of the man they saw building some houses near to the seashore. His fellow traveller was sceptical of Wigglesworth's opinion. Then they came to Blackpool, with its massive mountains of ocean waves mercilessly pounding the shore. There they saw a row of flattened houses. Forgetting his earlier comment, Smith's companion said, 'It's those sands. That's what it is.'

'We must have something better than sands,' affirmed Wigglesworth. 'Everything is sand except the Word.'

Faith's opposition

It is dangerous to look at Wigglesworth's life as a string of successes. 'If you are to be really reconstructed,' he would warn people, 'it will be a hard time... not in a singing meeting, but when you think there is no hope for you... tried by fire... God purges you, takes the dross away, and brings forth pure gold. Only melted gold is minted ...'

Once, when baring his soul to a group of American Bible School students, he confessed that he was 'continually confronted with things which God must clear away. Every day something comes before me that has to be dealt with on these lines.' He went on to relate how for three weeks a man who was stone deaf sat directly in front of him in every meeting. Not only did he take his seat on the front row, but he pulled it out into the aisles to make himself more conspicuous. Each meeting, morning and evening, when Wigglesworth would stand to preach and then pray for the sick, the devil would say, 'Now, you're done.' And Smith would reply each time, 'No, I'm not done.' The man was healed, and in a dramatic fashion. Wigglesworth was not even near him. The congregation was singing a hymn when the man became exceedingly distressed. He was erratically jumping about in all directions like a frightened animal. Suddenly he rushed out of the marquee and up into the nearby foothills. The rush of sound into his untrained ears at the moment he was healed scared him.

'Oh, the devil said to me for three weeks, "You cannot do it." I said, "It is done!" As though God would ever forget. As if it were possible for God to ever ignore our prayers!

'I believe that there is only one way to all the treasures of God, and it is the way of faith ... It is not crying, nor groaning. It is because we believe. Sometimes it takes God a long time to bring us through the groaning, crying, before we can believe ... Prayer changes hearts but it never changes God ... if you get anything from God you will have to pray into heaven for it is all there. If you are living on this earth and expect changes from heaven it will never come. If you want to touch the ideal you must live in ideal principles.'

And this was his novel conclusion to that particular address: 'Have you come out yet? You say, "Out of what?" Out of that you know you didn't want to be in.' Adding, somewhat impishly. 'Why should I answer your questions when you can answer them yourself? It would be a waste of time.'

19 And how was the Pope to know?

A Catholic Christian

'Kneel down here on the floor, and I will ask God to save you,' commanded Wigglesworth. And the young Italian priest did just that.

Smith was in Rome at the invitation of the Italian Pentecostal Church, and high on his recreational list was a visit to the catacombs. His guide was a young English-speaking Roman Catholic priest.

Wigglesworth was full of interesting questions which revealed that he knew more than the average tourist. Towards the end of the tour, by which time Smith and the young man had developed a rapport for each other, the priest commented, 'You would make a good Catholic, sir.' Quick as a flash Smith replied, 'I am a Catholic, but not a Roman Catholic.' Adding, 'Now, young man, you would make a good Christian if you were to get saved.' The Roman Catholic priest knelt on the stone floor and Smith Wigglesworth placed his hands on his head and committed him to the saviour. The priest was so overjoyed that he repeatedly kissed Wigglesworth's hands, and James Salter, who was accompanying him at the time, later said, 'It was only with great difficulty that he could get away from the young man's embrace.'

The words of a prophet

Not long after that incident Smith Wigglesworth was in South Africa as a guest of the Apostolic Faith Mission. The year was 1936, and an event that occurred then is still having an effect on the Roman Catholic Church over fifty years later.

It was not long after six o'clock on a gloriously sun-filled morning in Johannesburg, and the thirty-one year old General Secretary of the Apostolic Faith Mission, David du Plessis, was at his desk. He was in his efficiently equipped office at that hour to clear his desk of work so that he could give the rest of the day to his guest.

'I was bent over my desk, fully absorbed in a letter, when suddenly the door burst open,' said du Plessis. There had been no warning knock. In the doorway stood the commanding figure of Smith Wigglesworth. He stood there without a smile, erect and immaculate in his grey suit. Then, without a greeting or word of explanation, he pointed a finger at the South African minister, almost menacingly, and barked, 'Come out here!'

Without a question and without hesitation the Secretary obeyed.

With a no-nonsense attitude, Wigglesworth pushed him against the wall and, looking him straight in the eyes, began prophesying. David du Plessis was not unfamiliar with Smith Wigglesworth's unconventional methods of dealing with people. Smith was a guest at David's home, and David had travelled with him to most of his meetings, many times acting as his interpreter. But at this early hour he was, to say the least, just a little apprehensive. In addition, there was a sense of awe in the church office that early morning.

'I have been sent by the Lord to tell you what he has shown me this morning,' Smith said. 'Through the old-line denominations will come revival that will eclipse anything we have known through history. No such things have happened in times past as will happen when this begins.'

He went on, 'It will eclipse the present-day twentieth-century Pentecostal revival that already is a marvel to the world with its strong opposition from the established church. But this same blessing will become acceptable to the churches and they will go on with this message and this experience beyond what the Pentecostal have achieved. You will live to see this work grow to such dimensions that the Pentecostal movement itself will be a light thing in comparison with what God will do through the old churches. There will be tremendous gatherings of people, unlike anything we've seen, and great leaders will change their attitude and accept not only the message but also the blessing.'

Recalling this astonishing incident some years later, du Plessis said, 'Wigglesworth paused at this point, ever so lightly, as his eyes burned into mine.' Then, with measured tones, Wigglesworth added, 'Then the Lord said to me that I am to give you warning that he is going to use you in this movement. You will have a prominent part.'

There followed a further hesitation from Smith, albeit very brief, before he concluded his unique message to the younger minister with these words: 'One final word, the last word the Lord gave me for you. All he requires of you is that you be humble and faithful. You will live to see the whole fulfilled.'

He closed his eyes, bowed his head, and in a quiet voice said, 'Lord, I have delivered the message of what you are planning to do with this young man. And now Lord bless him and get him ready. Keep him in good health so that all this may come to pass. Amen.'

Without any further ado, the old man released the young man from his hold, stepped back a pace, turned on his heels and without another word was gone.

David du Plessis was stunned, flabbergasted!

The astonishing element here is not only the message but the person chosen to be God's messenger. 'Come out from among them' was the typical cry of the Pentecostals to Christians in other denominations, and Wigglesworth would not have been slow to encourage them in the doing. But here he was telling a young Pentecostal minister that he had to 'go in among them'.

As David was musing on this, there was a gentle knock on the door. It was Smith Wigglesworth again. With an

outstretched hand and a smile on his face he greeted du
Plessis. 'Good morning Brother David. How are you this
morning?' 'About now, very puzzled,' David replied. 'And
why is that?' Smith seemed surprised.

'Well now,' said David, 'you come into this office, and you
stand me against the wall, and you prophesy, and now you
come back in and act as if you'd never seen me before. And
you want to know why I'm puzzled?'

Quite unabashed, Wigglesworth explained that when the
Lord in olden times gave a message to the prophets he warned
them to 'speak to no man on the way'. And that is just what he
did. He even walked past Mrs du Plessis in the house on the
way to her husband's office and didn't say a word. 'But now
we can talk about it,' he said.

He related to David du Plessis the remarkable visitation he
had personally received from God that very day before
sunrise, in David's own home. In a vision he was given the
message he had just delivered. He added that he was, as one
would imagine, somewhat reluctant to accept it. 'That's not
what my brethren expect,' he told the Lord. The Lord replied,
'You must tell this to David, give him warning: he is to have a
prominent part in this.'

In reply to Smith's question, 'You've got it?' David assured
him, not without some trepidation, 'Yes, I've got it,' adding
somewhat thoughtfully, as he quickly contemplated the
future, 'I think I'll never forget it. But you'll have to
understand. I just can't accept everything you've said. If it's
going to happen and I'm supposed to get involved in it, then
the Lord will have to speak to me himself.'

'That's wisdom,' countered Smith. 'Don't act just on what I
or anybody else says. The Lord will tell you. But for now he
wants you to have this warning – because it's coming, that's
for sure. He will prepare you in the Spirit. But remember, it
won't come tomorrow. It will not even begin during my
lifetime. The day I pass away, then you can begin to think
about it. By the way, do you ever get airsick?' This was almost
too much for David. Very few people were privileged to fly

in those days. 'Do you ever get seasick?' Smith was with his questions again. David had not travelled by air or even by sea. And he told him so.

Once again the young man was instructed to stand before the ageing prophet, now well past seventy, who placed his hands on his shoulders and prayed for his life to be preserved in his travels by air and sea.

As Wigglesworth foretold, there were no dramatic events overnight. However, one thing came 'out of the blue'. Within three weeks of Wigglesworth's prophecy an airmail letter arrived from America, asking du Plessis if he would be one of the preachers at the Assemblies of God General Council for the following year (a prestigious event for an unknown South African minister).

David's own 'pilgrimage of faith' was to follow, and it was no rose petal pathway: financial hardships, a nomadic way of life, sacrifices galore, and finally rejection by his Pentecostal colleagues. But had not Smith described his message from God as a 'warning'? He also said that there were to be two essential elements, humility and faithfulness. In 1947 Wigglesworth died. David thought that was the end of the prophecy, forgetting that it signalled the beginning!

(I have given a brief account of my observations of the beginning of the charismatic movement in the historic churches in Appendix 2, 'And how was Wigglesworth to know?')

Did Smith smile?

In 1952 in Willingen, Germany, over two hundred Christian leaders who occupied strategic positions throughout the world's denominations assembled for a meeting of the International Missionary Council. David du Plessis was there as the 'Pentecostal friend' of the Rev Dr John Mackay, President of Princeton Theological Seminary and Chairman of the conference. During those eleven days he was besieged by more than half the delegates who would usually say, 'Okay now, start at the beginning and explain Pentecostalism to me.'

Describing the meeting in his book *A Man Called Mr Pentecost,* du Plessis writes: 'It was genuinely ecumenical, enough to bring a smile to Wigglesworth's face.'

You must read du Plessis' book to get the full story. He travelled and travelled, by air and by sea, never once becoming sick, talking to priests and ministers, moderators, presidents and bishops about 'Jesus the baptiser in the Holy Spirit'.

In his book you will read in detail how Wigglesworth's prophecy was fulfilled in a way which can only be described as miraculous. No human hand could arrange it that way. Imagine this message being transmitted to the Pope; 'Make the Bible available to every Catholic in the world – in his own language. If Catholics will read the Bible, the Holy Spirit will make that book come alive, and that will change their lives. And changed Catholics will be the renewal of the church.' David was in Rome, in the private apartment of Cardinal Bea and that was the message he gave to the Cardinal for the Pope.

'He stared straight at me,' said du Plessis. 'Then with a sudden move of his arm – in fact his whole body – he thumped the arm of his chair and bounced to his feet. "Now that's what the Holy Father wants to know!" He almost shouted. He swung abruptly toward Monsignor Schmitt. "Write that down. Yes, that's it! Write that down."'

The year was now 1976. Forty years after being given, Wigglesworth's prophecy was certainly being fulfilled, sometimes sensationally. But I doubt if our prophet could ever have foreseen what was to happen this year.

Again David was in Rome, this time he was attending the fifth and final session of the Pentecostal–Roman Catholic dialogue which had begun in 1971. It was a meeting of three classical Pentecostals, three main-line Protestants and three Roman Catholics.

'So you are Mr Pentecost?' the man completely clothed in a white cassock said.

'That's what they call me,' replied David du Plessis.

It was the Pope!

20 His last journey

The world's bitterest war was over, but its ravages were not. Casualties were strewn across life's fields like autumn's decaying leaves. As if in sympathy with this human plight and the bankruptcy of nature's resources, the north winds blew with icy severity during the short days and dark months of 1947.

The death of a servant of God

One of Wigglesworth's closest friends, who, I like to affectionately call 'Warrior Wilfred', a patriarch of Pentecost, had gone to his rest. And Smith would not miss this last opportunity to pay tribute to his compatriot of many years.

The journey to Wakefield from Bradford was tortuous. Yorkshire had suffered its heaviest snowfalls for many a year. James Salter had been asked to conduct Wilfred Richardson's funeral; so making sure his father-in-law was suitably clad for the inclement weather, they undertook the journey of some twenty or more miles.

The little church was packed to capacity. Richardson was a well-respected man of God. Salter assisted Smith Wigglesworth, who was now eighty-eight, through the church building to the small room used as a vestry for the ministers.

Smith warmed himself at the vestry fire and exchanged greetings with a ministerial colleague whose daughter had been ill. He had been asked to pray for her, and now enquired about her state of health. 'Well Brother Hibbert, how is she?' 'She's a little better, thank you,' the father replied. 'Her pains have not been so bad these past few days.'

Then Wigglesworth took his seat before the inviting fire, in surroundings he enjoyed. He was at home in his native Yorkshire, with some of his friends around him. He closed his eyes, sighed, and fell 'asleep'. A painless passing.

Was it just a coincidence?

When sudden death occurs in this country it is necessary for a post-mortem examination to be performed on the deceased. For no known reason, this did not take place for Smith Wigglesworth. He had refused the surgeon's knife many years earlier on more than one occasion. And he had told his wife, 'No knife will ever touch this body.' Was this another prophecy fulfilled, even in death?

An epilogue

When he was well advanced in years Smith Wigglesworth was invited by a representative group of Christian leaders, comprising many different denominations, to discuss the subject of church unity. They all came wearing their denominational badges. He had none. He did not, and had not belonged to any church denomination, although perhaps it could be argued that having been confirmed in the Church of England he had become a part of that church. However, he always refused to become a member of any religious denomination he attended or where he ministered – even the Assemblies of God, where he had his closest fellowship. So, in one sense, he was in a better position to speak of spiritual unity than any.

But he must have ploughed a few more furrows in the brows of the church dignitaries present when, in addressing them, he said: 'If I had all you have now before I received this, what is this I have received since and in addition to all I had when I had all you have?'

Then he gave this summary of his life of faith – his spiritual pilgrimage: 'I was saved among the Methodists when I was about eight years old. A little later I was confirmed by a Bishop of the Church of England. Later I was immersed as a Baptist. I had the grounding in Bible teaching among the Plymouth Brethren. I marched under the Blood and Fire banner of the Salvation Army, learning to win souls in the open air. I received the second blessing of sanctification and a clean heart under the teaching of Reader Harris and the Pentecostal League. I claimed the gift of the Holy Spirit by faith as I waited ten days before the Lord. But in Sunderland in 1907, I knelt before God and had an Acts two-four experience. The Holy Spirit came and I spoke with new tongues as did the company in the upper room. That put my experience outside the range of argument, but inside the record of God's Holy Word. God gave me the Holy Spirit as he did to them at the beginning.

'I want harmony, unity and oneness. But I want them in God's way. In the Acts of the Apostles, speaking with new tongues was the sign of the inflowing and outflowing of the Holy Spirit, and I do not believe that God has changed his method.'

And so it was that in the vestry of Glad Tidings Hall, Wakefield, Yorkshire on March 12th 1947, he died with a smile on his face.

A prayer for the Holy Spirit

Lord, I stand in need of oil. My lamp burns dimly. It is more like a smoking flax than a burning and shining light. Oh, quench it not, raise it to a flame!

I want a 'power from on high'; I want penetrating, lasting 'unction of the Holy One'; I want my vessel full of oil; I want a lamp of heavenly illumination, and a fire of divine love burning day and night in my heart; I want a full application of the blood which cleanseth from all sin, and a strong faith in thy sanctifying word.

In a word, Lord, I want a plenitude of thy Spirit, the rivers which flow from the inmost souls of the believers who have gone on to the perfection of their dispensation. I do now believe that thou canst and wilt thus baptise me with the Holy Ghost and with fire; help me against my unbelief; confirm and increase my faith. Lord I have need to be thus baptised by thee, and I am straitened till this baptism is accomplished.

Give me thy abiding Spirit, that he may continually shed abroad thy love in my soul. Come, O Lord, with that blessed Spirit! Come thou and thy Father, in that Holy Comforter! Come to make thy abode with me, or I shall go mourning to my grave!

Righteous Father, I hunger and thirst after thy righteousness; send thy Holy Spirit of promise to fill me herewith, to sanctify me throughout, and to seal me completely to the day of eternal redemption. Pour out thy Spirit on me till the fountain of living waters springs up abundantly in my soul, and I can say in the full sense of the words, that thou livest in me, and that my life is hid with Christ in God.

To thee, the first and the last, my Author and my end, my

God and my all, be the praise and the glory forever and ever, Amen.

(From a prayer of John Fletcher[1] of Madeley)

Note

[1] John Fletcher, a close friend and confidant of John Wesley, was born in Nyon, Switzerland, in 1729 but made his home in Madeley in Shropshire where he was Vicar of that humble parish. Voltaire, when challenged to produce a character as perfect as Christ, at once mentioned John Fletcher of Madeley.

Appendix 1

The Pentecostal baptism and tongues

Baptism

The late and venerated Dr Martyn Lloyd-Jones once gave me his definition of the baptism in the Holy Spirit: he described it as a spiritual experience which is separate from and subsequent to the new birth. In his view it did not have to be accompanied by speaking in tongues, whereas Smith Wigglesworth would insist that tongues was also necessary.

Some people take issue over the use of the word 'baptism'. They are prepared to accept the word 'filled'. However, the baptism in the Holy Spirit, allowing for further infillings of the Holy Spirit, is an essential part of Pentecostal teaching.

David du Plessis gives as good an explanation as I have seen anywhere: 'The Greek word "*baptizo*" can convey the sense of an act that is either repeated or permanent. But as I see it, when a ship dips up and down in the sea, it is "*bapto*". But when that ship is "*baptizo*" it is sunk. That's baptism – immersed permanently, buried with Christ.

'As for the baptism in the Holy Spirit, Christ immerses us in the Spirit rather than in water, and he leaves us there. We have to walk in the Spirit. That is our new life.'

Tongues

Acts 2 is the first significant reference to speaking in tongues following the baptism in the Holy Spirit. The early disciples 'began to speak in other tongues, as the Spirit gave them utterance'.

They spoke in languages they didn't know. They announced the wonderful works of God. Hence speaking in tongues was a language of praise and worship. It is significant also that this was the Day of Pentecost, one of the three chief Hebrew festivals which was 'the feast of harvest... first fruits'. It was a time of celebration, rejoicing and thanksgiving to God.

1 In three of the five accounts of the baptism in the Holy Spirit recorded in the Acts of the Apostles reference is made to 'speaking in tongues' as evidence that those present had received the Holy Spirit (cf. Acts 2:4; 8:12–19; 9:17; 10:44–47; 19:1–6; in Acts 11 and 15 Peter, referring to the events of Acts 10, compared them to his own experience on the Day of Pentecost, viz. 'as on us').

2 It is also a gift which, when used with the gift of interpretation, communicates divine truths to an assembly of believers. This elevates the gift to the level of prophecy whose purpose, according to Paul, is for 'exhortation, edification and comfort'.

I should make it clear that Wigglesworth distinguished between two of the ways in which 'tongues' are used: 1. as a once-only 'sign' at baptism (described as the 'initial evidence') and, 2. as an ongoing 'gift'. To the best of my knowledge the majority of today's Pentecostal leaders would not make such a distinction. They would look upon the 'gift' as the 'sign', so that everyone who has spoken in tongues may expect to continue to do so.

Speaking in tongues has other benefits for the believer. It stimulates growth in his spiritual life, and gives him the opportunity to express himself in the worship of God beyond the limits of his vocabulary.

In 1 Corinthians 14: 22 it is also described as 'a sign to the unbeliever'. This has puzzled some Christians.

This is my explanation: First, I do not believe that its use in this way is the norm. However, the Holy Spirit can cause it to happen as a mark of his authority in a given place. A 'sign' in the language of the Hebrew prophets is that which, to the person to whom it is offered, acts as evidence of the presence of divine authority. For example: 'Then Isaiah said, "Hear now you house of David! Is it not enough to try the patience of men? Will you try the patience of my God also? Therefore the Lord himself will give you a sign. The virgin will be with child and will give birth to a son, and will call him Immanuel"' (Isa 7: 13-14, NIV). To the shepherds visited by the angel at the time of the birth of Jesus they were told, 'this shall be a sign unto you' (Luke 2: 12, AV). Luke records that Jesus refused to give the people of his day a sign. As I see it, the use of the gift of tongues on these rare occasions can be the seal, sign or evidence of the authority of God given to that speaker and brings with it serious consequences if treated lightly.

Critics of speaking in tongues frequently accuse the speaker of merely using gibberish. Some have even attempted to analyse recordings in support of their criticism. However, for the earnest enquirer evidence is available of many instances when known languages have been used, which were unknown to the person exercising the gift of tongues. During my research for this book I came across a number of instances, and here are two, from different sources, and different parts of the world.

Browsing through the archives of the Assemblies of God, in the United States, I came across this record provided by the Rev Ralph Durham before he died in 1985: 'It was during one of these early revival meetings [1915] that I received the Pentecostal experience. A few months later my older brother Floyd also received the baptism and a call to the ministry. He went into Mexico for a week and preached in Spanish. The unusual part of the campaign was that Floyd knew no Spanish – the Holy Spirit spoke through him with great results.'

The year of the outpouring of the Holy Spirit at All Saints, Sunderland (1907), was to see a most unusual happening thousands of miles distant in the home of a noble Indian

Christian lady, Pandita Ramabai, in Mukti, India. A veteran missionary by the name of Albert Norton, accompanied by a lady missionary, was attending a prayer meeting in one of the rooms of the house, where about twenty Indian girls were praying. Presently he heard one praying very distinctly in English. He was completely astonished as he knew that, with the exception of his companion, no one present could speak English. 'I opened my eyes,' said Albert Norton, who was very close to the person speaking. 'Within three feet of me,' he continued, 'on her knees with closed eyes and raised hands was a woman whom I had baptised at Kedgaon in 1899, and whom my wife and I had known intimately since as a devoted Christian worker.' There were others, illiterate women and girls from Marathi, also speaking in fluent English and other languages. 'This was not gibberish,' said the missionary, who recognised different tongues without understanding them. 'I was as impressed as I would have been had I seen one, whom I knew to be dead, raised to life.'

The year before, in the Church Missionary Society Boarding School in Bombay, a sixteen year old Indian girl, when in prayer with three other girls, spoke in tongues. An Anglican minister, Canon Haywood, was called in. He was a wise man, not easily scared, and recognised this to be analogous to the Day of Pentecost. Bombay, being a cosmopolitan city, enabled the canon to make enquiries of people who understood a variety of languages. Eventually he was successful. Someone understood much of what the young girl was saying. She was pleading with God for Libya!

Appendix 2

And how was Wigglesworth to know?

'Apparently the heavenly Father's views of denominational barriers differ from many of his children. This occurred to me when I heard that Roman Catholic monastics in Germany were exercising the gifts of the Spirit and Plymouth Brethren in Britain were speaking in tongues. The present manifestation of the Holy Spirit may be the most important ecumenical event of our time.' So wrote the Warden of the Community of the Holy Spirit.

'God's frozen people' as Episcopalians are commonly known to their fellow Americans, were in the vanguard of 'the charismatic movement', as it was soon to be called.

Episcopalian priests came to London in the early 1960s, at the invitation of the Rev Michael Harper who, when curate at All Souls Church, London, had entered into his Pentecostal experience. I heard one describe the operation of the gifts of the Holy Spirit in their churches. Following the singing of the *Agnus Dei* in one of their services, there were utterances in other tongues, once by one of the altar boys and on another occasion from someone in the nave. These were promptly interpreted by the priest at the altar. There was no confusion. All was carried out in an orderly manner. It so happened that the diocesan bishop was present when this took place. When asked by the resident priest, 'What did you think of the service, bishop?' he replied, 'Quite orthodox, but rather long wasn't it?' It had lasted four and a half hours!

'News that Episcopalians were speaking in tongues was certainly strange: it sounded so incongruous! But it was

probably attributable to a flirtation, under the hot Californian sun, with the extravagances of pentecostalism...'
wrote Dr Philip Hughes in *The Churchman*. So he went off to
investigate.

This was all happening in the early 1960s, when I was
travelling throughout Europe generating interest in an
ecumenical radio station on behalf of the Swiss churches. My
points of call in countries scattered across Europe from
Norway to Spain, and Britain to Italy, were the offices of
priests and ministers of all the Protestant denominations. I
was then an Elim Pentecostal Church minister and carried
the 'handle' of 'Reverend'. Seated in a pastor's study, I was
usually asked, 'And what is your denomination?' When it was
known I was Pentecostal, questions about the work of the
Holy Spirit came tumbling out, cascading all around me. No
thought of my radio brief! And that is how I came to see the
need to alert my Pentecostal brothers of the hunger for the
fullness of the Spirit which I found all over Europe. And the
hunger was no greater anywhere than among my 'liberal'
friends.

Prior to this, David du Plessis had been quietly but
persistently foraging ahead, travelling the world, primarily
America and Europe, with his message, 'Jesus Christ; the
baptiser in the Holy Spirit.' Smith Wigglesworth's prophecy
was coming to pass.

'On Passion Sunday, April 3rd 1960, something occurred
in a staid, suburban Episcopalian church that rocked
religious circles the world over. Father Dennis J Bennett,
Rector of St Mark's Episcopal Church, Van Nuys,
California, with a membership of 2,500, announced in his
Sunday sermon that he had been filled with the Holy Spirit
and had spoken with other tongues.' This was reported in an
American magazine.

Dennis Bennett was asked to leave. A sympathetic bishop
offered him a rundown church some hundreds of miles away
in Seattle. It was about to fall under the bishop's dismissal
hammer because no one wanted to preach there, and very few

wanted to sit there. But it was the beginning of a Spirit-filled ministry that filled the church to bursting point and gave Bennett a ministry to the world. His book *Nine O'Clock in the Morning*, which I had the privilege of publishing in Britain and the Commonwealth, is still a best seller for my old company Kingsway.

Dennis Bennett, who has since become a faithful and much-valued friend, said this of his experience: 'After I became filled with the Holy Spirit I realised what had transpired and the significance of it... I naturally rejoiced in my experience and attempted to fit the experience into my theology and my devotional practices. To my astonishment, it did not fit. To my horror my theology began to change and it was most terrifying. The Holy Bible, which I had previously considered to be a history of the Jewish people plus an interesting follow-up that my church had written, suddenly became to me the living, breathing Word of the eternal Godhead. The body of Christ, which I had formerly believed to consist of the Anglican Church, the Roman Catholic Church and the Orthodox Church, became to me all those who had accepted Jesus as Lord... I enjoyed a new and exciting relationship with our blessed Lord that I previously sought through meditation and other devotional practices, but never quite found... Thanks be to God that he has not changed, and that the baptism of the Holy Spirit is still a reality for believers today.'

In 1964 I was invited by David Winter, now head of BBC religious radio programmes and then editor of the prestigious monthly, *Crusade*, to write about this new Pentecostalism. 'Today,' I wrote, 'less than four years later [than Dennis Bennett's announcement], we hear of Anglican and Methodists, Baptists and Presbyterians, Lutherans and Plymouth Brethren, who are opening their hearts and minds to this new movement of the Holy Spirit, which even in the fifties we would have thought impossible. Arthur Wallis (well-known and highly regarded in Plymouth Brethren meetings) at the Christian Convention in Eastbourne said, "A new movement is under way. God is creating in the hearts of many of his children a thirst for himself, for revival, for the Holy Spirit... God is meeting with Christians today, from churches, assemblies or independent fellowships, having no connection with the Pentecostal movement, and filling them with his Spirit as in apostolic times."'

These strange happenings compelled Bible scholars, theologians, priests in Catholic churches, ministers of other denominations and laymen to scrutinise the New Testament passages dealing with these occurrences.

Frank Farrell, then editor of *Christianity Today*, wrote, 'Not many months ago these same people showed relatively little interest in the subject, despite a half-century of aggressive promotion on the part of the Pentecostal movement, for the movement was outside the historic, mainline denominations. Now it is within, and clergy and laity have been driven to a probing of the scriptures and Church history, for answers to questions, and explanation of phenomena, pressed hard upon them by fellow ministers and parishioners.'

Time magazine carried reports stating that Pentecostals now 'outnumber traditional Protestants by at least four to one in most Latin American countries...' The writer added, 'These are facts which deserve our attention. There is no more significant phenomenon in the Church today than the attempt to rediscover the Person and work of the Holy Spirit.'

And so I could continue. But I must end, as this was only the fulfilment of but one part of Wigglesworth's ministry.

However, I must not conclude this account without the following up-to-date story, something which would not only have brought a smile to Smith's face but also a crackling chuckle to his ribs.

At the moment of writing I live in the delightful village of Capel in Surrey. Across the road from my cottage is the Methodist Church. Not many months ago, at the invitation of the Rev Trevor Nicholson, our vicar, a Roman Catholic priest, Father Bryan O'Sullivan, came from Egham to speak to us in the hall of that church, which had been kindly loaned for the occasion. The subject for our Epiphany meetings, chosen by the vicar, I might add, was 'Renewal'. It was an experience I shall never forget and one that gave me so much joy.

He told how he was disillusioned with the priesthood, and decided to resign. Before writing his resignation letter to his bishop he decided to go away for a contemplative weekend. There he came across Canon David Watson's book *One in the Spirit*. He was riveted to it. Then he read books by Canon Michael Harper and Colin Urquhart, as well as other books by Catholics such as Kevin Ranaghan. Returning home he searched out fellow Spirit-filled priests; this resulted in his personal baptism in the Spirit. He told of driving home in his car with the windows wide open, singing in the Spirit and enjoying the new scripture songs he had learnt. As the priest spoke I noticed the question marks on the brow of my good friend the vicar. I must confess they did amuse me!

Then Father O'Sullivan related a conversation he had had with Cardinal Suenens of Belgium, the most prominent charismatic in the Roman Catholic Church.

Cardinal Suenens had been in Rome for some renewal meetings along with some other Catholic charismatics. During their visit they were given an audience by the Pope. They happened to have with them a video of one of their charismatic meetings, and the Pope expressed a desire to see it. It was arranged. The Pope watched with rapt attention as priests and lay people danced in the Spirit and spoke in tongues to the glory of God. Their joy was evident by the expressions on their faces. At the conclusion, the Pope rose from his seat and began rearranging the chairs in a circle. When someone dared to ask him what he was doing, he replied that he would like them to repeat in his presence what they did in their own meeting, just like that on the video. And Wigglesworth? That would have brought a smile to his face.

MADAME GUYON

Phyllis Thompson

The story of Jeanne de la Mothe Guyon is a remarkable one. An apparently ordinary wife and mother living in seventeenth-century France, her deep love for God and her unswerving Chritisn commitment stirred up hatred and opposition in the highest political circles of her time. The spread of her simple teaching on the love of God, the abandonment of self-centredness and the acceptance of God's will brought Madame Guyon imprisonment and interrogation, but she remained devoted to her Saviour to the end.

'To write her story has been a fascinating task,' says Phyllis Thompson. 'Relevant, instructive and challenging... the message she proclaimed does not alter with the times.'

'A well-spring of inspiration.'   *The Friend*

Presents the life and message of a special soul in very readable fashion.'   *Church Times*

Phyllis Thompson is the author of many popular books, including *The Gideons, To the Heart of the City* and *An Unquenchable Flame.*

ONLY THE BEST

Noreen Riols

A true and absorbing family saga spanning over a hundred years, *Only the Best* is the entertaining story of Noreen Riols' large and colourful family.

From her much-travelled Uncle Freddie, with his energetic monkey and vociferous parrot, to her wayward son-turned-anarchist who set up his own 'parallel school', from her autocratic and terrifyingly charming grandmother to the grandchildren she so delights in looking after, Noreen's world is alive with humour and energy.

Not glossing over the buried hurts and hidden guilt that so often underlie family life, Noreen's story highlights the mother's key role in shaping the future, and affirms that what all parents want for their children is what God wants for every person: 'only the best'.

Noreen Riols is author of *Eye of the Storm* and *Abortion: A Woman's Birthright?*

THE LOCUST YEARS

Jacqui Williams with David Porter

A chance encounter in a San Francisco bus station introduced Jacqui Williams to a community that was to change her life. Instead of going home, Jacqui, a young British Christian on holiday in the States, became a member of the Unification Church. In less than three months, she was convinced that the Revd Sun Myung Moon was the Messiah.

Jacqui's dedication – and success – were astonishing. Within two years, she was top fund-raiser for the 'Moonies', following a punishing schedule of hard sell and mission work that took her all over the United States and Canada. But when disillusionment and doubt set in, friends were at hand to point the way to a new life of true freedom, acceptance and love.

Jacqui Williams is now an active member of her local church and a primary school teacher in Bracknell, Berkshire.

David Porter is a freelance writer and journalist. He is the author of many books, including *Children at Risk*.